SHARPHAM MISCELLANY

SHARPHAM MISCELLANY

ESSAYS IN SPIRITUALITY & ECOLOGY

Edited by
JOHN SNELLING

TOTNES
THE SHARPHAM TRUST
1992

Contents

John Snelling died shortly before this book went to press

Editor's Introduction

THE SHARPHAM ESTATE consists of some five hundred and fifty acres of gently hilly farmland and woodland in the South Hams district of South Devon. Its heart, Sharpham House, was designed in the Palladian manner around 1770 by Sir Robert Taylor, who also worked at the old Bank of England and at Lincoln's Inn Fields, and its building financed with prize money won by a freebooting naval captain named Philemon Pownoll. It stands on a commanding bluff overlooking the River Dart. On one hand, the river flows down to Dartmouth and the sea; on the other hand, the eye follows it up across wetlands to the old river port of Totnes, much, one sometimes feels, as Sir Lancelot's eye followed another river up to Camelot in Tennyson's 'The Lady of Shallott'.

Totnes today is a centre of alternative culture; but long ago, if we are to believe Geoffrey of Monmouth, it was the place where the Trojan champion Corineus fought Gogmagog, the last of the British giants. Corineus must have carried the defeated leviathan past Sharpham on his way to Plymouth Hoe, where he finally dashed him onto the rocks of the sea. This struggle between an old and a brave new race, reminiscent of the clash between the Titans and the Olympians of Greek mythology, is an apt association for an estate that today is dedicated to a number of bold experiments in agriculture and social living oriented towards the integration of all aspects of life in a new organic unity.

Accordingly one finds here large tracts of land farmed according to the Biodynamic theories of Rudolf Steiner, a vineyard producing grapes for the dry Sharpham wine, and a Jersey herd whose milk goes into the Sharpham, Ashprington and Elmhirst cheeses that are made here along with the Beenleigh Blue moulded sheeps'-milk cheeses. In addition there is a working retreat centre, the Barn, where up to nine residents, staying for up to six months, can integrate working on the land with meditation and community living, while the upper floors of Sharpham House itself now accommodate the Sharpham North Community, whose members, drawn from different backgrounds and nationalities, share an interest in meditation and its application in daily life. The community also takes care of an organic vegetable garden and runs a comprehensive programme of talks, meditation sessions, retreats and workshops.[1] Finally, the Sharpham Trust, the charity that nurtures most of these activities, also sponsors a programme of conferences, seminars and colloquia where in-depth discussions are held on matters like the transmission of Buddhism and the other Eastern religions to the West, new directions in philosophy, psychology and the arts, ecology and allied concerns.[2]

The present volume contains transcribed talks and papers by those who have in recent years participated in either the Sharpham North programmes or in the Sharpham conferences. Of necessity it represents only a very small selection of the available material but nevertheless should give the reader a fair idea of the range of subjects and viewpoints that have been aired in these contexts.

Though neither the Trust itself nor any of its ancillaries holds any special allegiance to Buddhism—nor to any particular religious school or sect for that matter—Buddhism features prominently here, and for a good reason. Our present global predicament is the direct result of the way we are presently constituted, in particular the way we think. Unfortunately, our analytic

---

[1] Those wishing to know more about events at Sharpham North are invited to write for a current programme to the community at Sharpham House, Ashprington, Totnes, South Devon TQ9 7UT.
[2] A brief survey of the conferences held to date appears at the end of this book.

and reifying processes destroy the seamless unity of nature and inaugurate instead a fallen world of separate 'things', which are set against one another, manipulated and exploited, with the devastating results that we see all around. Everyone agrees that something is deeply wrong but all attempts to save the situation by reforming externals seem at best to provide only temporary symptomatic relief. While outward action (to protect the environment, promote peace, redress social inequities and so forth) is certainly necessary, what has not been considered to any significant extent hitherto is the possibility of tackling the problem at its root: in the way we think and consequently behave. Logic tells us, however, that we cannot reform thought by thinking; that would be much the same as to try to save a sinking ship by pumping more water into its hold. What then to do? This is where Buddhism comes in, for its traditional texts not only speak of a source of wisdom beyond thought, one that is synthetic or holistic and so conduces to consciousness of the interconnectedness and interdependence of all that exists, but also offer a repertoire of practical methods or techniques for gaining access to that wisdom.

The Indian philosopher Nagarjuna, for instance, the seminal master of the Madhyamaka or Central Way school, devised a devastating dialectical method that could, by showing the ultimate absurdity of all propositions, oblige the practitioner to relinquish all views and thereby arrive at the enlightened state. In this he anticipated the modern linguistic philosopher Ludwig Wittgenstein by around seventeen hundred years, for Wittgenstein too, by remorseless analysis, arrived at the outer limits of what can be significantly said and hence thought— at which point, he suggested, the person who understands his propositions aright would transcend them; he would kick them away, as a person kicks away a ladder he has used to climb up to a new level, and then 'he will see the world aright'.[3] A practical

---

[3] Ludwig Wittgenstein, *Tractatus Logico-Philosophicus*, translated by D.F. Pears and B.F. McGuiness, London, 1961, p.151.

transformative method that is more widely used, however, is sitting meditation practice, which is, as we have noted, a central feature of the life of the Sharpham North Community, but something that is done there, not in a rarefied spiritual vacuum, but within a matrix of ethical and philosophical values, and alongside the earthing activities of running a community on a day-to-day basis, tending a garden, earning a living and relating to a diversity of farming and allied pursuits.

Those who wish to know more about the ideas underpinning what is going on at Sharpham could do no better than to read the opening piece in this miscellany, 'Philosophy of Sharpham' by Maurice Ash, who with his late wife Ruth bought the estate in 1962 and whose family home it continues to be. It is Maurice Ash's own deep concern to find a way out of our contemporary impasse that has inspired all the various interrelated activities described here.

Thanks to Jan Hartell for her help in transcription and proof-reading.

John Snelling
Sharpham North
July 1990

A NOTE ON STYLE

As this is a miscellany and in consequence contains a variety of articles, ranging from the relatively academic to those addressed to a more general readership, I have not attempted to impose a standard style in the matter of the spelling, accenting and italicization of foreign language terminology but instead have allowed each writer to adopt his or her own procedures.

J.S.

Philosophy of Sharpham
Maurice Ash

INITIALLY I HAD WANTED TO TALK only about the idea of
Sharpham—about what might be achieved on this particular
estate—but of course the philosophy underpinning that idea
goes much deeper. A comparison comes to mind with the idea
of Dartington, the experiment which Leonard Elmhirst started
more than sixty years ago. As he told it: 'I went to the estate agent
and said, "What sort of place have you got?" and he said, "What
do you want—hunting, shooting, fishing?" I replied, "No, none
of those"'—and, as it turned out, that was almost the sum of
what Leonard was ever prepared to discuss concerning what lay
behind the multi-faceted idea of Dartington.

I think that was admirable for its time—for, after all, what is
there to be said about the very ground of our existence?—but
those were times, in 1925, when the model of the past could
still be taken as the given against which to compare oneself.
Dartington seemed so radical then, and was so much resisted,
largely by contrast with that model. But for us, nowadays, the
past has collapsed; its values cannot even be mocked. The paradigm has shifted, and Sharpham is part of that shift.

So I have felt it right to take seriously the philosophy in which
the idea of Sharpham lies embedded. Seriously—but not too seriously; for not only am I not a philosopher, but I don't really know
what philosophy is. I would only subscribe to Wittgenstein's
notion that the aim of philosophy is to guard against the bewitch-
ment of our intelligence by language. I think this means, in

practice, you should not expect from me any grandiose statement of ideals; nor, indeed, of any ideals at all.

I do not know if I need to justify here my judgement that we are living through the collapse of a whole system of values—and perhaps do so by reference to the anomie that underlies the manifold incohesions of our society. But this has been spoken and written of *ad nauseam*—maybe, since the world still has not in fact come to an end, even till it comes up against a barrier of scepticism. So I must just content myself now with saying that such moments have indeed been known to history, most notably with the decline and fall of Rome, a period of crisis in Western culture with disturbing similarities to our own. Then, too, there was a crisis of authority, for the old gods were failing (just as our belief in material progress is declining today) and, like today, all manner of new cults were growing. Inflation in Rome between AD 250 and 275 was of the order of three thousand per cent, and in the next century became even higher. It is all ominously familiar.

Recently, I came across this quotation from the *Soliloquies* of Marcus Aurelius, who was Emperor in the second half of the second century:

> Yesterday a drop of semen, tomorrow a handful of spice and ashes. In the life of man his time is but a moment, his being an incessant flux, his senses a dim rush light, his body a prey of worms, his soul an unquiet eddy, his fortune dark, his fame doubtful. In short, all that is of the soul is dreams and vapours; an empty pageant, a stage play, flocks of sheep, herds of cattle, a pusillanimous spearman, a bone flung among a pack of curs, a crumb tossed into a pond of fish, ants loaded and labouring, mice scared and scampering, puppets jerking on their strings; that is life.

Spengler or Nietzsche could hardly have said it better!

I have mentioned a crisis of authority in our culture. The authority I have in mind is that of knowledge. Our kind of knowledge, in whose thrall we lie, is reductionistic; it derives from taking things apart in order to examine them. And the crisis in this knowledge lies in our not understanding how they should be put together again. We owe this knowledge to the likes of Newton and Leibniz, and all who followed them. Philosophically speaking, however (though Newton and Leibniz would have repudiated this, which must tell one something about philosophy: at least, about the philosophy of philosophy), this idea of what knowledge is stems from Descartes—and is consequently known as Cartesian. Descartes, however, only completed the dualism inherent, at least since Plato and the Greeks, in the Western tradition and perpetuated in Christianity: the dualism between material and spiritual, essence and appearance, good and evil, body and soul, etc. Cartesianism, then, only codified this tradition through the duality of the world and the self: the self being, in Descartes' system, a substance of which the only purpose was to think. This philosophy sanctioned the gap in logic between observer and observed, whilst measurement of the world's extension was treated as a kind of sacred thread across this divide—for 'God would not deceive us' about it.

Nowadays, of course, we are beginning to realize that this very notion of knowledge is flawed. The observer is not separated from the observed, and the certainty presumed by any detached observation has been supplanted by our recognition of Nature's inherent indeterminacy. From this has developed an acceptance of wholeness as a tenable and alternative kind of knowledge, in contrast to the atomism of reductionistic thought. It has become acceptable (even if only modestly so) to see the wood for the trees. We are all in favour of the environment!—which is as much as to say that the kind of knowledge by which we have hitherto set all our store is bringing upon us consequences, such as the greenhouse effect, which are in fact beyond its comprehension.

Yet there is nothing so very new about this derogation of knowledge. Again (and not surprisingly so) contemporary with the fall of Rome, St Augustine said: 'Without charity, knowledge inflates; that is, it exalts man to an arrogance which is nothing but a windy emptiness.' Analogously, what the so-called Enlightenment has meant by knowledge has generated the spiritual vacuum in which we find ourselves today. The fragmentation of our knowledge has brought a loss of meaning for the knower; at the same time as the self through its knowledge has become more conscious of itself, it has lost any context for this knowledge—leaving its own existence meaningless.

In reaction against the nihilism implicit in this situation, there has been a swing towards so-called 'holism'. I think, however, a word of warning should be heeded here. This is prompted by a recognition that advocates of an organic, or ecological view of the world may sometimes, and with some justice, be accused of fostering a new ideology, one that is just as intolerant as the other ideologies that have bedevilled our century. Indeed, I am very conscious of having experienced the rise of Fascism in my youth and of how seductive then was its claim to be 'organic', or (and the word was coined at that time) 'holistic'. This element of tyranny has been characteristic of all utopias, from Plato's *Republic* down to the present day. There is, indeed, a profound fallacy in any notion that a whole of any kind can be completely self-justifying. This, I think, is what caused Wittgenstein to say (in the *Tractatus*): 'Feeling the world as a limited whole—it is this that is mystical.' You will not be surprised to learn, then, that my notion of Sharpham has nothing to do with self-sufficiency.

But it does have to do with spirit. Spirit is what limits any whole, for in itself it is unaccountable. In Wittgenstein's terms: 'The meaning of the world must lie outside the world.' Or as St John put it: 'The spirit is like the wind that bloweth where it listeth: and whence it cometh and whither it goeth, you know not.' In this, spirit is akin to causation, for, as David Hume explained two hundred years ago—and Buddhism knew two thousand years ago—causation is mysterious. (It was not for nothing that Jupiter was the god of causes.) We are in the midst of it, but at best we can only infer what it is from our habits or from statistics.

Yet is this not but another way to speak about environment? For environment is not just another thing 'out there', in dichotomy with the self. (At least, this is so if we are not talking about not-in-my-backyard environmentalism, which would turn the environment into a chattel.) Environment, rather, is the ground of any disparate thing—whence it comes and whither it goes. It is uncreated form, and not least 'the fury and the mire of human veins'. But to reify an environment is for it to cease to be an environment. Thus, to speak truly of environment is to give spirit a home; and, likewise, spirit is that without which matter has no meaning. Anyone at all knowledgeable about Buddhism, then, will I think see the affinity of environment, thus understood, with 'emptiness', the end of all dialectic, when there is no thing for another thing to refer to—except the language itself we agree to use: and not least, therefore, the disappearance of any notion of a substantive self. And I think this helps account for the yearning for spiritual fulfilment that underlies today's interest in environment.

So I too am coming to the end of what I can usefully say about the philosophy in which, for me, Sharpham is embedded. It ends in silence: in the realm of meditation, therefore, which occupies a central place in this philosophy. Needless to say, however, this implies no commitment to what I think has been called 'spiritual materialism': to the mastery of any ritual, or even an attachment to non-attachment. For those like myself, then, who find meditation the hardest practice in the world—being, perhaps, indissolubly set as we are in the old cast of mind—let me recommend Gerard Manley Hopkins' poem:

Elected silence, sing to me
And beat upon my whorlèd ear,
Pipe me to pastures still and be
The music that I care to hear.

Shape nothing lips; be lovely-dumb:
It is the shut, the curfew sent
From there where all surrenders come
Which only makes you eloquent. . . .

and so on through its several verses. You can read them for your-
selves. I cite this poem—and I might just as well have cited the
slow movement of Schubert's *Quintet in C*—because, more than
any reasoning, it illustrates for me the vital role of meditation in
any philosophy we try to live.

So to conclude with Sharpham itself and how it might fit into
any such scenario, it must be obvious I am supposing a very
different kind of world from the present. To call Wittgenstein
once more in aid: 'The whole modern conception of the world
is founded on the illusion that the so-called laws of nature are
the explanations of natural phenomena.' A world in which this
was no longer true would be almost unimaginably different. Yet a
path is becoming clearer all the time. It is the way of seeing things
whole, rather than in fragments, but with the spiritual strength
of knowing that we can never see the whole completely; and an
estate such as Sharpham remains an excellent proving ground
for such a programme. It could act as a modest pioneer of the
new paradigm.

Sharpham, after all, has adapted before, and it could adapt
again. You can see it in the stones. The house, with its *piano
nobile*, is Palladian, with all the vestiges of sacred architecture
—of a house built to imitate the structure of the universe—which
that implies. But the great whorl of the staircase at Sharpham,
with its elliptical form, is Newtonian, not Renaissance: restless,
not passive like the primordial form of a circle. And, just by

occupying the central space of the house, the stairway has already isolated the house from the land, for the ground floor is no longer available, as traditionally it was, to store the produce of the land. The countryside has become merely a park to be observed from the house. Indeed, you can see on the rustication of the ground floor how the windows were altered (quite logically) even as the house was being built, to conform to the new pattern of life. And, of course, the village of Ashprington was built (in the neo-Classic style, forsooth) simultaneously with these changes to house the people displaced by the crime of the Enclosures and to allow of the rationalization of agriculture.

So, and not only to redress that crime, Sharpham will change again. The justification for its continuance at all is that it has a role to play in the reinspiration of the countryside. This role is not merely a return to the monastic institutions that played this part for so long in Europe after the catastrophe of Rome. If there are to be monks at all, they should surely be monks in the world. But there is indeed a new kind of renaissance to be fostered: not one that rediscovers the lost classical world, but rather the world that was lost sight of when, equally long ago, it took a radically different course from the one that in the West is now running into the sands.

I do not imply by this that the hidden agenda of Sharpham is to proselytize for Buddhism. I think it is enough just to open the West up to the East; we cannot predict what then might ensue. But in the ever-dubious realm of statistics, I treasure a favourite measurement. In an investigation into the religion of the Japanese it was discovered that ninety-two per cent were Shinto, and eighty-eight per cent Buddhist! In principle, I do not see why the same pattern should not come about in the Christian West. It is not Christianity itself that would pose the difficulty; some forms of early Christianity were remarkably Buddhistic. The Church and Original Sin, rather, might pose a little problem. (Islam, however, has always managed without a Church.) But, seeing in recent times how great empires have faded away like morning mist before the sun, we should not allow ourselves to be discouraged.

Meanwhile Sharpham is in trust, and will remain so. This is the only way in present circumstances to ensure that land is not just a chattel to be possessed. This is not a question of stewardship of the earth, which seems to me a typically presumptuous, humanistic notion. Rather, it bears upon our dualistic cast of mind and the possessiveness intrinsic to the idea of self so basic to that dualism. If and when it becomes recognized that the value of land is due, not so much to the use any owner makes of a piece of it, but rather to what happens all around it, to its context, a different form of land-holding with its attendant taxation will no doubt be endorsed by a different frame of mind. Till then, trusteeship may seem a rather feeble stop-gap, but it will suffice.

Making the Connection
Jonathon Porritt

I WANT TO TRY AND EXPLORE a problem relating to the word 'ecology' and the way it is being used today, because it has struck me for a long time that there is a real contradiction at the heart of the matter which is often not worked through at all.

I well remember when I first joined the Ecology Party, which is what the Green Party used to be called, we used to receive anguished letters from professors of ecology, saying how dare we use the word 'ecology' in this imprecise way. They were implying that because we weren't trained ecologists with the right collection of letters after our names we hadn't the right to call ourselves ecologists, and therefore the Ecology Party was a complete and utter hoax. This was always extraordinarily baffling to most of us, who weren't trained ecologists but nevertheless didn't think that ecology was the exclusive domain of those who happened to see it as a science.

That was my first brush with the complications of using the word 'ecology', but it became a much deeper issue for me when debate was joined within the Ecology Party itself as to whether or not it was appropriate to talk about a spiritual element in Green politics and whether to make that just as important a part of our platform as, say, the campaigns for lead free petrol and against acid rain. This came to a head at the 1983 General Election when we were writing our manifesto. Even in a small party a manifesto is a highly controversial matter, and it became even more so in 1983 when those of us involved with drafting the document decided we wanted to have a major section on the spirit. This gave rise to a wonderful debate that I suppose had been lurking below the surface for a very long time. Some people got very worked up and said that it was no part of the activity of a serious political party to concern itself with the spirit, but a larger number said 'Thank God!'—or the appropriate non-denominational alternative—that we were at last getting down to the bedrock of what green politics is about. And eventually, when it was actually in the manifesto, a lot of people were very interested in the idea that there was some connection between politics and spirituality. I'm not talking here about the kind of connection one finds in Northern Ireland, but of one concerned with the relationship between human beings, and between people and planet.

I have, however, learned from experience that it's very difficult to talk about the spiritual aspects of green politics without falling into all sorts of traps. The Green Movement itself is now going through a very interesting phase of development in that it is trying to show that it is respectable. After years of having been dismissed as mere 'muesli munchers' and all the rest, we are now trying to establish a place for the Green Movement at the heart of the highly conventional political decision-making process—the Establishment, if you like—and one of the things that is not acceptable there is to combine your politics with a sense of spirituality, let alone to talk about it in any open or straightforward way.

To give you a small example, I can recall the sense of utter mystification I felt at a very interesting meeting with local Euro-MPs outside Farringdon. It was a rather boring meeting really, just ticking over, until someone on the platform told a very interesting story of how on his way there it had been a beautiful spring evening and he had knelt down, thrust his hands into the earth and let it trickle through his fingers. He then asked: 'To what extent does this experience affect your views on the Common Agricultural Policy?' It was quite a poser, so I suggested, while I formulated my own thoughts, that another person on the platform should try to answer it. He was a very conservative MEP, a very interesting and intelligent man who was an expert on agriculture and food and European matters generally, but he suddenly went into the most defensive overdrive imaginable, letting loose a barrage of fears and concerns about environmentalists.

'Well, this has been a very good and sensible meeting up to now,' he said, 'but this merely confirms my fears that you people in Friends of the Earth are a bit strange.'

He then went on to describe his fears that the Green Movement was tapping into the same emotional power that the Nazis has exploited in the 'Thirties: the same sense of reverence for the earth, love of forests and rivers and so forth. Admittedly the original question had been tricky, but it shouldn't have induced that kind of panic. Also, had that question not been asked we would have been in danger of spending the whole evening talking about Common Agricultural Policy and agriculture generally without ever evoking any sense of relationship with the earth.

That was very interesting for me in pointing up the problems inherent in trying to combine conventional political theorizing with the much more radical connections that we in the Green Movement are trying to draw between our politics and our relationship with the planet. There's really a fundamental philosophical challenge here, for we largely stand apart from the dominant Western materialist philosophies that tell us that the world is made up of discrete objects separate from each other—Cartesian and Newtonian reductionism, and so forth. We feel those views do not accurately convey a sense of what the world is about, nor do they give us an opportunity to express the full potential of the human spirit.

Aldo Leopold, one of the most astonishing writers on ecology who worked before the upsurge of ecological thinking of the 'Sixties and 'Seventies, describes land (which was his shorthand word for the environment) as a fountain of energy flowing through a circuit of soils, plants and animals. This notion that life is really not a matter of disconnected objects but a flow of energy in which any one object or series of objects may have a transient part to play is obviously something that touches the base of the philosophy of ecology today. And that philosophy moreover rejects the concept of a separable self or ego: the notion that there is self and there are others. And it goes further than that to undermine the whole notion that there is actually any fundamental separation between ourselves and all other living organisms on the planet. Now that is an enormously important part of the policy of ecology but also a very important part of the spirit of ecology as well.

It is, of course, very easy to say these things but hard to live them. I for one went around for years with a theoretical concept of what interconnectedness meant, and got a great deal of reassurance from it, but living it, feeling it—that's a different matter. In fact, there isn't any single prescription for living it. Different people arrive at it in different ways. Almost everyone who becomes a committed Green tends at one stage or another to have an experience or series of experiences in which the connection between him or herself and the earth has made a particularly startling if not searing impression. Then, instead of it being a comfortable, theoretical abstraction it becomes a living reality.

In my own case, looking back, I did all my preparatory reading about ecology (though there wasn't that much to read in those days, and much of what there was was written in a kind of American jargon that was disturbing to one's aesthetic sensibilities) and thought that I was an absolute whiz-kid in all the theory of ecology, but in fact I was still a complete and utter idiot. It wasn't until I spent nine months in New Zealand planting exotic pine trees—which is not actually a terribly ennobling occupation if you do it day after day in the wind and the rain—that I began to develop what I can only describe as a living relationship with the earth and to feel enormously committed to developing that relationship. I was lucky enough to be living in a hut on the property and nobody else came to bother me, so I experienced that loneliness that is very nourishing and formative. Nearby there was an extremely beautiful ten-acre tract of native bush that had somehow escaped development. The local people refered to it as the Cathedral, which was very appropriate because there were tall, straight Kauri and Rimu trees which actually gave you a sense of being in a cathedral. The combination of tree-planting and having connections with this place, where I felt very strongly the spirits of the earth moving through me, was my turning point as an ecologist.

So if that hadn't happened I might well have gone on thinking of myself as an ecologist but in all honesty I wouldn't really have been living it in the way that I now feel I can and sometimes do. Actually, the fact that the way one has to live as Director of Friends of the Earth[1] does not leave a lot of time for this kind of experiencing is a source of deep regret to me. I find it an enormous contradiction that there I am, spending most of my life talking about the importance of relationships between people and planet, about more opportunities for reflection, about gentler and more caring ways of life, and, to be honest, the forty minutes that we've just spent meditating is probably the first time I've thought about the deeper issues for about four or five months. That is the peculiar state that many of us in the Green Movement find ourselves in now. We've become so obsessed with doing that we've often given up on the being, and there is a real danger in that.

I want to end by talking briefly about the implications of this for what is happening in the Green Movement today. What I'm really trying to explain is this notion of one organism on earth and of ourselves as temporary functions in a very complex flow of energy. Now, the concept of interdependency is in my

---

[1]This paper is based on a talk given at Sharpham North Community in 1986, when Jonathon Porritt was Director of Friends of the Earth.

view absolutely central to the breaking down of the barriers that vitiate our political processes today. Unless one is able to explain, particularly to children, how we have a stake in, for instance, the world's rain forests, in the famine in Ethiopia and whatever else it might be, unless we can trace for them the threads that interweave our lives with the lives not only of other people but other organisms and other habitats in different parts of the world, then I see us condemned to narrow forms of nationalism and parochial politics.

I have for years felt extremely hesitant about internationalism as propounded in some political ideologies. They seem to be suggesting a peculiarly narrow form of linkage—between members of one class (to use the appropriate jargon) across national boundaries. That never seemed to me to tap into what internationalism is really about, which is the concept of one people, one family—whatever you like to call it—on one earth. The ecological principle of interdependency therefore assumes a far greater importance than merely explaining to children what the food chain might mean or how it is that we are linked with other organisms. It points in a very direct and immediate way to the fact that the damage we cause the planet is damage done to ourselves. That's its political importance. The other part of it, as I've explained, is the spiritual one: the importance of seeing oneself as a living part of that enormously complex flow of energy that is the planet. Without acceptance of this spiritual dimension I am really in very grave doubts as to whether ecology will make much of a difference to the future of the planet.

There is at the moment a school of ecology that is all to do with managing our environment more efficiently and effectively. In the document known as 'The World Conservation Strategy' the notion surfaced that what ecology was really about was doing better what we had been doing up to now, which was using the planet instrumentally in order to meet the very specific needs that we, as the dominant species, have. We would simply have a slightly re-geared relationship with the planet and, because we would be doing things so much more efficiently, there wouldn't be a problem any more.

Now, I find myself, in Friends of the Earth, very conscious of the fact that we sometimes play to that version of ecology in our Rainforest Campaign, when, for instance, we are up against what we would consider to be a hard-nosed audience. When I go into a school almost the first point I make is to try and show the kids how they have a stake in the rainforest by telling them that one in every four products they would find in a chemist's shop would have originated in the rainforest and about the way those drugs have benefited us. I use all kinds of words like 'asset' and so on, and even as I'm saying that I am conscious of falling into what I consider to be a very dangerous instrumental view of ecology which merely sees the future in terms of the more efficient management of natural resources.

In 'World Conservation' this was touched upon with particular force in relation to saving the whale. In a really extraordinary passage it talked about the ethics of saving the whale and why the whale should be seen as different from other species which we use and often abuse in order to fulfil our needs. What is the distinction between a whale and a cow when it comes to killing? It went on to talk about the success of the various pressure groups, Greenpeace, Friends of the Earth, the International Whaling Commission and others, in almost stopping commercial whaling. Next it said that if the moratorium on commercial whaling works as well as everybody hopes it does it is perfectly possible that the populations of the different endangered species of whales will be restored in a relatively short period of time, say, ten to fifteen years. Finally, it asked what happens at that point. Why should the whaling industries then not get back into business, managing the whales as a sustainable resource, i.e. a resource that we can use if we do so in such a way as not to threaten its long-term survival?

Of course, the instrumentalist concept of sustainability is one that is utterly devoid of any ethical or spiritual meaning. That, I think, is the point that the debate has now reached. In the next couple of weeks we are going to see the launch of the report of the Bruntland Commission, which was set up two or three years ago to report on the ways in which development in Third World countries could be organized so as to preserve the wealth of their fragile environments, not only to meet the need of this generation but to protect it for the future as well. That's suddenly been called 'sustainable development' and everyone's talking about it now rather than about ordinary development. It might be though that this constitutes a real move forward in the debate about the relationship between ourselves and the planet. Well, at one level it truly does. Don't get me wrong, I am delighted that at long last the aid agencies and government bodies like the Overseas Development Administration are realizing that unless development is compatible with ecosystems you can't call it development at all. At best you can call it anti-development, because it really isn't helping people in any significant way. But it goes no further than that. It doesn't touch this spiritual notion of the relationship between ourselves and the planet.

What I'm really saying is that the thinking about these issues is moving fast and it's very encouraging to see the extent to which it's penetrating all sorts of places where one might not have assumed it was going to reach for many years. Yet there is a grave danger that those who are in the business of taking over these ideas and using them for their own purposes may well be persuaded that because they have learnt to wrap their tongues around the words 'sustainable development' and their minds around a few easily-accessible Green concepts—and have been coached in a little 'Greenspeak' to boot—that the goals that we are after have actually been achieved.

So I feel very, very strongly that the Green Movement needs right now to be making itself clearer on this more complicated but much more important issue of the relationship between ourselves and the planet, and that means talking in a way that is still frightening to much of the conventional Establishment, with whom we have to do business. So I'm tossing down a challenge to all of us to put spiritual concerns up front. We don't have to call them spiritual concerns if that's going to create an automatic defence barrier, but there are ways of talking about things that do not allow us to fall into this instrumentalist trap of thinking in terms of simply managing our natural resources more efficiently.

Buddhism and Meister Eckhart

Maurice Walshe

THE THOUGHT of the great German Dominican mystic
Meister Eckhart has been compared more than once with the
teachings of Buddhism, especially Zen (and also with Vedānta).
It may be as well to recall, very briefly, his career. Eckhart was
born about 1260 at Hochheim in Thuringia and entered the
Dominican friary at Erfurt about 1275. He rose rapidly in
his Order and was sent several times to Paris, where he took
his Master's degree and later taught and debated. It should be
stressed that all else aside he was a highly qualified theologian
with the scholastic philosophy of his day at his finger tips, and
that the Dominicans were considered the special upholders of
orthodoxy. It was only after about 1323, when he had been
appointed head of the great Dominican Studium Generale in
Cologne, that any suggestion was made that his views were
in any way unorthodox. At this time the aged Archbishop of
Cologne was busily engaged in hunting down heresy, particularly a somewhat amorphous group called the Brethren of the
Free Spirit. Apparently some of these people, arraigned for
their lives before the Archbishop, in desperation appealed to
the authority of the famous Dominican master. The Archbishop,
who was a Franciscan, instituted proceedings against Eckhart
for misleading the common people. Eventually the case came
before the Papal court, then at Avignon, and thither Eckhart
went to defend himself, all the while declaring his orthodoxy,
The case dragged on, and Eckhart died, no doubt at Avignon,
about the end of 1327. In March 1329 Pope John XXII issued

a bull in which twenty-eight of Eckhart's propositions were denounced, some as definitely heretical, some as under suspicion of heresy. I hasten to add that the modern representatives of his order believe Eckhart was wrongly condemned, and the Pope has been asked to set the matter right. In due course we may hope that this will happen. There may be some who are—let is say romantically—surprised and even disappointed to learn how vigorously Eckhart protested his orthodoxy, and that those best qualified to know are in agreement with him. But that is by the way . . .

Another preliminary remark I should make is that until recently there has been—and to some extent still is—doubt about the authenticity of certain works ascribed to Eckhart. Much earlier work, especially in English, was based on material that was dubious or spurious—including the charming tale of 'Sister Cathy'. Latterly, this situation has changed, and many books have been written on the basis of more accurate knowledge. My own translation is based on the monumental edition of the original texts, as far as they could be certainly authenticated, by the late Professor Josef Quint of Cologne. However, I will as far as possible spare you boring technicalities.

It may be useful to introduce Eckhart to you backwards, as it were, with what may well be his parting words to his pupils before setting out for Avignon. They are found in a text which I feel is authentic:

> Meister Eckhart was besought by his good friends: 'Give us something to remember, since you are going to leave us.' He said: 'I will give you a rule, which is the keystone of all that I have ever said, which comprises all truth that can be spoken of or lived. It often happens that what seems trivial to us is greater in God's sight than what looms large in our eyes. Therefore we should accept all things equally from God, not ever looking and wondering which is greater, or

higher, or better. We should just follow where God points out for us, that is, what we are inclined to and to which we are most often directed, and where our bent is. If a man were to follow that path, God would give him the most in the least, and would not fail him. It often happens that people spurn the least, and thus they prevent themselves from getting the most in the least, which is wrong. God is in all modes, and equal in all modes, for him who can take Him equally. People often wonder whether their inclinations come from God or not, and this is how to find out: if a man finds it within himself to be willing above all things to obey God's will in all things, provided he knew or recognized it, then he may know that whatever he is inclined to, or is most frequently directed to, is indeed from God.

Some people want to find God as He shines before them, or as He tastes to them. They find the light and the taste, but they do not find God. A scripture declares that God shines in the darkness, where we sometimes least recognize him. Where God shines least for us is often where he shines the most. Therefore we should accept God equally in all ways and in all things. Now someone might say: 'I would take God equally in all ways and in all things, but my mind will not abide in this way or that, so much as in another.' To that I say he is wrong. God is in all ways and equal in all ways, for anyone who can take Him so. If you get more of God in one way than another, that is fine, but it is not the best. God is in all ways and equal in all ways, for anyone who can take Him so. If you take one way, such and such, that is not God. If you take *this* and *that*, you are not taking God, for God is in all ways and equal in all ways, for anyone who can take Him so. Now someone might say: 'But if I do take God equally in all ways and in all things, do I not still need some special way?' Now see. In whatever way you find God most, and you are most often aware of Him, that is the way you should follow.

But if another way presents itself, quite contrary to the first, and if, having abandoned the first way, you find God as much in the new way as in the one you have left, then that is right. But the noblest and best thing would be this, if a man were to come to such equality, with such calm and certainty that he could find God and enjoy Him in *any* way and in *all* things, without having to wait for anything or chase after anything: *that* would delight me! For this, and to this end, all works are done, and every work helps towards this. If anything does not help towards this, you should let it go.

I have in my translation noted an external parallel to Buddhism here by pointing out that the words 'God is in all modes, and equal in all modes' are repeated with the hammer-blow effect of a Buddhist *sutta*. In many a sermon, Eckhart has described the birth of the Word in the human soul and other mysteries. Here, in his final exhortation he is insisting on what his disciples ought to *do*. It is above all the essence of his *practical* teaching—which to my mind argues strongly in favour of its authenticity. As regards Buddhism, I long ago ventured to coin the phrase: Buddhism is not something to *believe* but something to *do*, and it is here in the practice, or in the practical attitude, that Eckhart's teaching and Buddhism seem to come especially close.

It would of course be easy, in a superficial kind of way, to dismiss the whole of Eckhart's teaching as irrelevant to Buddhism simply because he speaks of God, which Buddhism notoriously doesn't. Some people may argue that this is not just a superficial or vulgar objection, but one of substance, pointing to a fundamental difference, an unbridgeable gap, between Buddhism and Christianity, and at one level it must be conceded that they have a case. I think it is best to deal with this troublesome point right away. Just because we want to be frightfully ecumenical, or frightfully high-minded, we should not try to gloss over what may be perceived as a real difficulty by some. It is good Christian doctrine, amply subscribed to by Eckhart in his inimitable way, that God is ineffable and beyond the normal range of human thought. Much the same is said by Buddhists about Nibbana, or the Unborn. Therefore, whatever may be the case with great sages and saints, we ordinary Buddhists and Christians, when we speak of God or Nibbana, literally do not know what we are talking about, and most of us are prepared to admit the fact. 'There is, O monks,' said the Buddha, 'an Unborn, Unbecome, Unmade, Unconditioned. If there were not this Unborn . . . there would be no deliverance here visible from that which born, become, made, conditioned.' While this statement (which has been variously interpreted), does not in the Buddhist view imply a personal God, it could be interpreted as so doing. In fact in Indonesia, where a religion to be recognized must be theistic, some Buddhists have used this 'Unborn' passage for the very purpose of legitimizing their faith in the eyes of the authorities.

Eckhart did not enjoy the freedom of thought prevalent in ancient India. Like the Indonesian Buddhists of today, only far more so, he had to conform outwardly. Until he landed up in Cologne, this may have been no great problem, but as soon as he encountered the persecuting Archbishop he was in trouble. He was far too important a man to be sent to the stake, but the Archbishop aimed to discredit and silence him—and largely succeeded. It is not to Eckhart's dishonour to say that he was compelled to work within the system with all the restrictions that implied. To have deviated too obviously from orthodoxy would simply have meant martyrdom, not only for himself, which he might have been willing to face, but for his followers. I am not, for instance, suggesting that Eckhart believed in any form of reincarnation or the like. I am merely saying that if he had any such belief he would necessarily—and sensibly—have kept quiet about it.

The comparison of Eckhart's thought with Buddhism has hitherto been really only made with Zen. The question is whether this was really due to an affinity with Zen in particular, or because the two writers to make the comparison were themselves Zen Buddhists: D.T. Suzuki writing in English, and Shizuteru Ueda writing in German. This question is perhaps of less importance than might seem, especially since the miasma of misinformation—and worse—about Zen itself has begun to lift, and it has become increasingly apparent that despite certain idiosyncracies Zen is after all not so different from other schools of Buddhism, and even—believe or not—Theravāda Buddhism, as many have thought. And since Theravāda is the Buddhist school with which I am most familiar, it is to that that I will relate rather than to Zen.

The constant burden of Eckhart's sermons is above all the birth of the Word in the soul—a theme which he repeats over and over again with variations. In his theology the Word is the Son, the Word spoken by the Father in the silent depths of the soul. There is, Eckhart says, and the proposition was among those condemned, something in the soul that is not created. Sometimes he calls it a castle, sometimes a spark. This spark (*scintilla animae*) is, in so far as it is pure divine intellect, uncreated and one with God, but as 'a power of the soul' it is created, being an analogue of the uncreated intellect. According to Eckhart, who here differs from St Thomas Aquinas, being is a property of God alone—hence his statement condemned in the bull: 'All creatures are mere nothing.' This is of course closer to Vedānta than to Buddhism.

I have said that Eckhart could not introduce some new and unorthodox doctrine—such as reincarnation, supposing he believed in it—without disaster. Similarly, he could not totally pass over anything in the official teaching that he might not have approved of. The most he could do was play it down and refer to it as little as he decently could. There was one such doctrine that he does seem to have treated in this fashion. It has been observed that there are remarkably few references to Hell in

Eckhart's writings, and those there are are pretty perfunctory. In this he differs notoriously from a whole range of popular preachers from his day to our own. The awful doctrine of eternal punishment derives from the Bible and was rigidly believed in by the Church of his time and later. Indeed, it was this frightful teaching that was responsible for all the tortures and persecutions of the Inquisition, for witch-hunts, and for untold misery and despair for untold numbers of believing Christians throughout the ages. Though it is ascribed to Jesus, personally, without being a Christian, I find it impossible to believe that he taught any such thing. If he did, he was worse than the Pharisees, who took a less extreme view. Of course there are some pretty frightful descriptions of hells in the Buddhist scriptures, but though long-lasting they are not said to be eternal, and they are not the creation of a loving father. In any case we don't have to believe in them in any literal way—though it can be assumed that those guilty of really nasty behaviour will have cause to bitterly regret it in some future existence.

We can, I think, usefully draw a parallel between Eckhart and Nāgārjuna, arguably the greatest Buddhist philosopher. Eckhart said, 'To get at the kernel, you must break the shell,' but if he too recklessly broke his orthodox shell, he was soon in trouble, whereas Nāgārjuna, in the vastly freer atmosphere of ancient India, could say what he liked without fear of suppression. There were many legends about Eckhart until modern scholarship turned up a few facts, and there were and are a good many legends still current about Nāgārjuna, some of which were even propagated—inadvertently of course —by modern scholars. One otherwise excellent book about him was by a Vedāntist who tried to make out that his views were those of the Vedānta. Others have held that he introduced a total revolution in Buddhist thought, breaking away from the earlier tradition. In fact, as has recently been shown, he restored the true teaching which had got garbled by the Sarvāstivādins, whose so-called Hinayāna beliefs have been wrongly ascribed to the Theravādins. I don't propose to go into all that here. What I am trying to suggest is that perhaps Eckhart was attempting, as far as he was able and as far as he was allowed, to restore something of the true doctrine of Christianity which had got more than somewhat overlaid by his time. Eckhart and Nāgārjuna were both deeply learned in the traditional systems of their respective orthodoxies. Both had, I believe, penetrated through the jargon surrounding the kernel of their faith and were concerned to bring it to light. In this, as I have said, Nāgārjuna was free to speak and write as he liked, which he did with incomparable dialectical skill, whereas Eckhart had to proceed vastly more cautiously.

Eckhart knew very well that some of his sayings would shock, even while he firmly maintained their orthodoxy. In the preface to a Latin work he wrote that many things he said might appear at first sight 'monstrous, dubious or wrong', and in his Cologne defence he said ironically that he was only surprised that his accusers had not adduced hundreds of other passages against him. Here is a passage from a sermon which contains two things his listeners had to reckon with. Neither was quoted against him, at least in the surviving records, but both may have occasioned some head-shaking, or scratching. He says there are two kinds of birth: birth *in* the world and birth *out of* the world, which is spiritual birth in God. He goes on:

> Christ says: 'Whoever would follow me, let him deny himself and take up his cross and follow me', that is to say: 'Cast out all grief so that perpetual joy remains in your heart.'

Probably few people would have interpreted this particular text (Matt.16.24) in just this way, though in context it is not illogical. But while his hearers are puzzling out this riddle, he delivers the shock:

Thus the child is born in me. And then, if the child is born in me, the sight of my father and all my friends slain before my eyes would leave my heart untouched. For if my heart were moved thereby, the child would not have been born in me, though its birth might be near.

Father and friends stand here for objects of attachment, to whose loss we should be indifferent.

We have a parallel in the *Dhammapada* 294:

Having slain mother, father, two warrior kings and having destroyed a country together with its revenue officer, ungrieving goes the Brahmin.

In the next sentence Eckhart explains his meaning:

I declare that God and the angels take such keen delight in every act of a good man that there is no joy like it. And so I say, if this child is born in you, then you have such great joy at every good deed that is done in the world, that your joy becomes steadfast and immutable . . . For we see that in God there is neither anger nor sadness, but only love and joy.

We can compare, I think, in Buddhism the 'opening of the Dhamma-eye' whereby the reality of Nibbāna is seen for the first time. Those in whom, in Eckhart's terminology, the Word is born, or those in whom the Dhamma-eye has opened, perceive reality and are transformed by it. Whether the impersonal reality of Nibbāna and the supra-personal Godhead of Eckhart's teaching are the same or not is not a question I would venture to discuss.

The nearest Eckhart ever came, or could have been expected to come, to criticizing the Church was when he said: 'If God could turn away from the truth, I would cling to truth and abandon God,' with the implication that if the Pope or the Church could abandon truth . . . And one thing that strikes us strongly is the assurance with which he speaks as one possessed of divine wisdom. This in itself is, of course, no proof of his wisdom or enlightenment—all too many people down to the present day have spoken with the authority of those who know, and all too often the outcome has been deplorable. But somehow, when Eckhart speaks, it is different. Some may think him mad, as the English Franciscan William of Ockham did, but to others his message rings clear and true. He is like a great beacon to lead those who wish to follow on the path to truth, albeit on a particular course not entirely of his making. It might be fair to suggest that he it was who plotted a path out of the labyrinth of medieval scholasticism. Buddhists have on the whole had it easier, and though at times they have doubtless been led astray by some of their teachers, they have at least not had to face the horrors of Inquisition and persecution for having gone astray, whether in reality or in the imagination of their spiritual superiors.

It is of course the Buddhist claim—according to certain scriptural passages which are probably of late date—that the truth of enlightenment, that leads to Nibbāna, is only revealed by buddhas, who appear at vast intervals of time. This may of course be quite true, but I somehow doubt it. It would of course be the height of folly, as well as supremely tactless, to debate about the possible relative degrees of 'enlightenment' attained by, say, the Buddha Gotama and Jesus. I think, however, that it is perhaps permissible to say that Jesus himself, like his disciple Eckhart only more so, was unlucky in his audience. The Buddha lived to be eighty and was never persecuted, though we are told of real or alleged attempts on his life. The transmission of his message was not so perfect as we could wish, and has left his followers— and modern scholars—quite a few things to argue about, but it certainly seems a great deal less dubious than that of the message of Jesus. I may remark in parenthesis that a distinguished New Testament scholar with whom I was once acquainted, and who died recently, was reported to have produced, on the basis of his research among the manuscripts, a new version of the New Testament that was so radically different from current versions that it was only published privately, in a limited edition, for his friends. I don't know what he found out, or believed he had found out, and haven't seen the book—and if I were to see it it would probably strain my poor knowledge of Greek to the limits and beyond to attempt to understand it—but it *may* be that it contains some new—and seemingly disconcerting—insights into the mind of Jesus.

What is enlightenment? Silly question—not being enlightened I can't tell you, and don't propose to try. Perhaps, however, it is possible to hazard a theory about the mechanics of 'disendarkenment'. Let us start with an analogical case in which not indeed enlightenment, but certainly some remarkable powers of the mind have been revealed. An interesting article in the *Independent* entitled 'Brilliance in a Benighted Mind' discusses the cases of some people who, despite grave physical and/or mental handicaps, yet display powers far beyond the capacity of most of us. A blind man suffering from cerebral palsy can play any tune faultlessly on hearing it only once. An animal sculptor with an IQ of about fifty and a vocabulary of about fifty words needs only a fleeting glance at a picture to be able to reproduce it in perfect three-dimensional detail. A twelve-year-old autistic boy drew an accurate architectural sketch of St Pancras Station after a brief visit, and so on. The author refers to left- and right-hand brain halves, the possible effect of hormones, etc., all of which may be perfectly true without going very far towards explaining the phenomena. Of course we now know that one function of the brain is to act as a kind of sieve through which the vast mass of sense-impressions passes to enable us to cope without being overwhelmed by them. The brain, in fact, is not so much a memory as a forgettory. It seems to me that these people have, as it were, a hole in some odd corner of the sieve through which some knowledge streams unhindered. The knowledge is unconscious and unselective, and certainly cannot in any way be equated with 'enlightenment', but it is genuine knowledge or skill of a high order, often with an aesthetic quality about it. It also seems clearly to contain, often at least, an element of extrasensory perception. In passing, I would like to suggest that it is questions such as these to which science should pay much more attention than it does. The time has surely come by now to stop brushing scientifically inconvenient facts under the carpet. Anyway, the phenomena I have mentioned, though clearly not themselves forms or aspects of 'enlightenment', may well be considered as possibly analogous to it.

The arising of the Dhamma-eye is described in the *suttas* as follows: 'And just as a clean cloth from which all stains have been removed received the dye perfectly, so in the Brahmin Pokkharasāti (or whoever), as he sat there, there arose the pure and spotless Dhamma-eye, and he knew: "Whatever things have an origin must come to cessation (*Yam kiñci samudaya-dhammaṃ tam nirodha-dhammaṃ*)"'—at first sight an almost trivial-sounding statement like 'What goes up must come down'. We may even think, too, of the Devil's version of Goethe's *Faust*: '*Alles, was entsteht, ist wert, daß es zugrunde geht*'—'Whatever comes into being deserves to perish'. Perhaps its profounder significance begins to dawn when we contemplate another 'celebrated verse', as Rhys Davids calls it:

Aniccā vata sankhārā uppāda-vaya-dhammino
uppajitvā nirujjhanti tesaṃ vupasamo sukho—
Impermanent are compounded things, prone to rise and fall,
Having risen, they're destroyed, their passing truest bliss.

said to have been uttered at the Buddha's passing-away by Sakka, king of the gods, and often quoted. The transience of all mundane things—things not of this world alone but even of the highest heavens—is here pointed up sharply, and the bliss of non-attachment to them is stressed. This is not full enlightenment but the moment of stream-entry or First Path, after which full enlightenment is certain. This latter comes with the total destruction of the *āsavas* or 'corruptions'. I have already suggested that the opening of the Dhamma-eye is comparable to the birth of the Word in the soul in Eckhart's terminology. About a century before Eckhart, Wolfram von Eschenbach, the greatest medieval German poet, wrote what I consider the finest version of the Holy Graal story, *Parzival*, which can be read in a fine Penguin translation by my friend Arthur Hatto. For Wolfram, uniquely, the Graal was not the chalice of the Last Supper or anything of that sort, but a stone which had come down from Heaven. The French scholar René Nelli thought that Wolfram drew on astrological conceptions of his time for his idea of a precious stone fallen from heaven which, by grace, had kept its pristine purity, thus participating in the incorruptible nature of the firmament. It is thus a (mythical) physical symbol of that spark in the soul of which Eckhart speaks, that is incorruptible and uncreated. Surely what Eckhart, and the Buddha, and Wolfram von Eschenbach are pointing to is the same knowing, differing only in degree—most completely in the Buddha, and perhaps if we could only find it, equally in the teachings of Jesus, less profoundly but very poetically in Wolfram. It must be, too, what my own venerable teacher, Ajahn Cha, calls establishing the Buddha in our mind, the Buddha being not the historical Gotama but 'the one who knows'—somehow impersonal and formless, but attainable if we make the effort and truly seek. This should of course not be literally taken to suggest that the Buddha is something like a personal God who knows—which would naturally be quite alien to the Buddhist way of viewing things and utterly foreign to the Ajahn's way of thought. 'The Buddha', he says in a *A Taste of Freedom*, 'is just this "One who knows" within this very mind! It knows the Dhamma, it investigates the Dhamma. It's not that the Buddha who lived so long ago comes to talk to us, but this Buddha-nature, the "One who knows", arises. The mind becomes illumined.' Are he and Eckhart, using different but not totally dissimilar words, groping towards an expression of the same thing? For Eckhart, understanding is the most important thing—he even differed from St Thomas in placing God's understanding above His being.

Conventional Buddhist wisdom would have it that Ajahn Cha, for instance, could be—indeed doubtless is—on the Path, whether as Stream-Winner, Once-Returner, Non-Returner or even Arahant. Eckhart on the other hand, not having been exposed to the teaching of Dhamma and being rooted in a theistic tradition, could not, it would be said, have even 'entered the Stream'. I think all that shows is that people who set much store by statements of that kind have themselves not made much progress along the Path, however learned they may be. They are blind like Eckhart's accusers. I don't profess to know whether Eckhart had reached First Path, or Second Path, or whatever, but I think he was further along the Path than many professing Buddhists.

I think by now I have interposed myself and my probably foolish opinions sufficiently between Eckhart and you. I will conclude therefore by allowing him to speak for himself. In an eloquent passage in his 87th Sermon he says that which should provide you with ample food for thought—and meditation. Eckhart says:

> Now pay earnest attention to this! I have often said, and eminent authorities say it too, that a man should be so free of all things and all works, both inward and outward, that he may be a proper abode of God where God can work. Now we shall say something else. If it is the case that a man is free of all creatures, of God and of self, and if it is still the case that God finds a place *in him* to work, then we declare that as long as this is *in* that man, he is not poor

with the strictest poverty . . . So we say that a man should be so poor that he neither is nor has any place for God to work in. To preserve a place is to preserve distinction. Therefore I pray to God to make me free of God, for my essential being is above God, taking God as the origin of creatures. For in that essence of God in which God is above being and distinction, there I was myself and knew myself so as to make this man. Therefore I am my own cause according to my essence, which is eternal, and not according to my becoming, which is temporal. Therefore I am unborn, and according to my unborn mode I can never die. According to my unborn mode I have eternally been, am now and shall eternally remain. That which I am by virtue of birth must die and perish, for it is mortal, and so must perish with time. In my birth all things were born, and I was the cause of myself and all things: and if I had so willed it, I would not have been, and all things would not have been. If I were not, God would not be either. I am the cause of God's being God: if I were not, then God would not be God. But you do not need to know this.

A great master says that his breaking-through is nobler than his emanation, and this is true. When I flowed forth from God, all creatures declared: 'There is a God'; but *this* cannot make me blessed, for with this I acknowledge myself as a creature. But in my breaking-through, where I stand free of my own will, of God's will, of all His works, and of God himself, *then* I am above all creatures and am neither God nor creature, but I am that which I was and shall remain for evermore. There I shall receive an imprint that will raise me above all the angels. By this imprint I shall gain such wealth that I shall not be content with God inasmuch as he is God, or with all His divine works; for this breaking-through guarantees to me that I and God are one. *Then* I am what I was, then I neither wax nor wane, for then I am an unmoved cause that moves all things. Here, God finds no place *in* man, for man by his poverty wins for himself what he has eternally been and shall eternally remain. Here, God is one with the spirit, and that is the strictest poverty one can find.

If anyone cannot understand this sermon, he need not worry. For so long as a man is not equal to this truth, he *cannot* understand my words, for this is a naked truth which has come direct from the heart of God.

None of Eckhart's accusers, so far as we know, made any reference to this passage. I commend it to you for your contemplation.

Who Speaks Through the *I Ching*?
Martin Palmer

THE *I Ching* IS WITHOUT DOUBT one of the world's oldest and most unusual books. Parts of it predate 1,000 BC and its basic form was extant by around 300 BC. As one of the Five Classics of Ancient China, the *I Ching* has exercised a remarkable influence over that country since around 200 BC.

In recent decades the *I Ching* has become the object of great fascination to the West. While the number of actual translations has been small, the number of books based upon them has been immense. The book can indeed be said to have spawned a whole cult or subculture in the West, even to the extent of many bookshops now having a special *I Ching* shelf. Extraordinary claims have also been made for it. For instance, I have been told in all seriousness that it can only answer really profound questions once, so were you to ask, 'Will the world destroy itself with nuclear weapons?', and someone else has already asked that, you will not get an answer!

But who or what is it that speaks through the *I Ching*? This question seems rather crucial to me. In seeking to answer it I want to turn from the plethora of 'translations' and books based vaguely on the *I Ching* and return to the people who have used and studied the book for over three thousand years, namely the Chinese.

The first thing to recognize about the *I Ching* is that its style —cryptic and at times frankly meaningless statements which require interpretation—is far from unique in Chinese literature.

It stands within a long tradition of similar writings and interpretations. This is important to understand.

The earliest written materials in China were oracle bones. Sometimes the shoulder bones of oxen or, more frequently, turtle or tortoise shells, were asked a question; then a small dent was made into which was placed a smouldering stick that heated the shell; the resulting cracks were then 'read' for an answer to the question. This was the origin of Chinese characters. Often the cracks, which were seen as pictures, gave rather vague readings which were meaningless unless interpreted by a shaman or some other expert. For instance, in the *Shih Ching*, one of the other Five Classics of Ancient China, there is a description of this process. In the section, 'Greater Odes of the Kingdom', there is a poem which describes the way in which the ruler T'an Fu led his people to a new site for their city in the year 1325 BC:

> The plain of Chou looked so rich and beautiful.
> Its celery and sowthistle as good as dumplings.
> Here we will start, here we will seek advice;
> Here mark our turtle shell.
> It says, 'Stop'; it says, 'This is the time.'
> This is where we shall build our homes

Now, one of the oldest legends associated with the *I Ching* is the story of Fu Hsi and the discovery of the Eight Trigrams. The Eight Trigrams, when combined, make up the Sixty-four Hexagrams, which are the very core of the *I Ching*. Fu Hsi is literally the all-purpose father of Chinese culture. He is credited with inventing just about everything: agriculture, marriage, cooking, language and many other essentials; he also taught humanity civilization. But his greatest claim to fame is the discovery of the Eight Trigrams. Legend tells us that as he was walking one day beside the sea a heavenly turtle emerged from the waters and there marked on its shell were the Eight Trigrams. Fu Hsi duly noted these down.

In sites across China oracle bones or shells have been found. There can be no doubt therefore that the Fu Hsi story fairly accurately reflects the origins of the Eight Trigrams and of Chinese language generally, even if it did not all arise in such a pristine state from a primeval sea. It also shows us that the messages from such oracles were generally rather vague and required understanding within a given context. As far as the practitioners of these ancient oracles were concerned, they were acting as messengers between the spiritual world and the physical world.

By the time the *I Ching* began to accrue its series of cryptic messages and interpretations (around 1,000 BC), a more developed philosophy had begun to emerge about where the messages came from. 'T'ien' is the phrase usually used to describe this source. It is the Chinese word for heaven, though we must banish from our minds anything that equates this with the Western Christian notion of heaven. In pure Chinese philosophy, heaven is the ultimate reality of which earth is a counterpart, but on a lower level. Heaven comprises all the cosmic forces and realities which actually constitute reality and is the source of all being. But, most importantly, heaven is not a god or any kind of divine being. It is not even really a divine place as such. It denotes simply the forces which, by following natural laws, ensure the continuation of existence.

From this strange mixture of oracle, spirit world/physical world and the emerging philosophy of T'ien came the texts of the *I Ching*, which as I have already stressed, were, like the rest of the vast corpus of Chinese divinatory or fortune-telling material, rather vague and requiring of interpretation. For instance, here is the text of Hexagram 30, *Li*, from the *I Ching*:

To part. It is useful to stand firm and behave well. This will bring success. Take care of the cows. This will be good fortune.

Compare this with the following extracts from two very popular oracle books in use throughout the temple systems of the Chinese diaspora:

> Lot 7. Your way ahead is blocked and barred. The streams bearing earth and red clay. If you explore in foreign places you'll find no work, no home to rest. (from the *Readings of Kuan Yuan*)
> Lot 93. The music of the states of Cheng and Wai was harsh to the ear; its melodies filthy, obscene like a poisonous spear. So different were they from the tunes of the old days; many a man was lost, many a town fell in its morbid ways. (from the *Oracles of Wong Tai Sin*)

No Chinese reader of the *I Ching*, the *Kuan Yin* or the *Wong Tai Sin* would dream of trying to interpret the readings without professional help. This, to put it cynically, is why the readings have the form they do. They are the basic tools of the diviner's and the fortune-teller's trade. Which is not to say that they are not 'divine' or originate from T'ien; but it is to say that they have manifested themselves within the context of a particular culture and have become the property of a particular group or trade.

One of the most famous stories associated with the development of the *I Ching* seems to reinforce the diviner's angle. The story goes that King Wen, the ruler of a small state in ancient China around 1,000 BC, was arrested by the invading army of the Shang dynasty. While in prison he wrote down the basic lines which describe the attributes of the sixty-four Hexagrams. After a year he was released and, although his lands were not restored to him, he was allowed to live in liberty.

Now, there are two interesting aspects to this story. Obviously, before King Wen wrote them down, the hexagrams did not have a set arrangement of texts to accompany them. They were presumably left up to the individual skills of each diviner. The second item of interest is: why did King Wen write them down? Our theory is that he used his divinatory skills to impress the rulers of the Shang dynasty so as to get them to release him as a 'wise man' who could render them assistance in such vital matters. After all, in the Bible we have a similar story of the use of divinatory powers not only to secure a release from prison but also to achieve a considerable betterment of status: the story of Joseph and Pharaoh's dreams in Genesis 39-41.

Let me stress again that by observing the human use and context of these hexagrams and their messages I am not saying that they are not important, or that they are not in themselves vehicles for messages coming from a source greater than ourselves. What I am saying is that, like any other human construction, be they buildings, languages, or philosophies, it carries with it the marks of those who shaped it regardless of what the original may have been.

After King Wen, his son King Tan added the commentaries on the individual lines of the hexagrams. Thus the essential features of the *I Ching* as we have it were in place by 1,000 BC—so much so, in fact, that the classic was originally known as the *Chou I*, meaning 'Changes of Chou', Chou being the name of the dynasty founded by King Tan which succeeded the Shang.

Now we come to a very strange period in the life of the *I Ching*. From 1,100 until around 213 BC it virtually disappeared from sight. The odd reference to it under its title of *Chou I* leaves us with very little solid data. With one extraordinary exception, not a single luminary of Chinese history, philosophy, or religion mentions the book: Lao Tzu, Mencius, Hsun Tzu, Chuang Tzu—all are silent about it. In the early lists of the Confucian Classics, moreover, instead of the *I Ching* we find a lost book called the *Yo Ching* ('ching' means 'book', by the way). It is not until the Burning of the Books under the tyrant Shih Huang-ti in 213 BC that the book emerges as a recognized classic of Confucian thought. This is rather odd. For the only figure in Chinese history from 1,100 to 213 BC who mentions the book is Confucius himself! Indeed, he not only mentions it, he is quoted as saying that if he was given extra years to his life he would devote fifty of them to the study of the *Chou I*. At another point he makes a direct reference to Hexagram 32.

So strange is this sudden appearance of the *Chou I* that some scholars have concluded that the texts must be later additions. I do not think so; but it is certainly odd that, while Confucius could speak so highly of the book, it was ignored by all his contemporaries. What we can categorically state is that the so-called 'wings' or expanded commentaries are not by Confucius himself but were probably written by his followers during the period 400 to 200 BC. They would have been assisting the gradual acceptance of the book by their peers in claiming that the wings were actually written by Confucius himself.

From the beginning of the Han Dynasty (207 BC) until the present, the *I Ching* has had a major, indeed pre-eminent position within Chinese culture and is the only one of the Five Classics still in everyday use by millions of Chinese. I cannot really expand upon that now, but I should instead like to move on to the emergence of the text in the West and look at the way it has been understood, or rather mis-understood, here.

When Jesuits serving at the Chinese court in the 17th century first encountered the *I Ching* they were totally baffled, for it offended their vision of Confucian China as a place of order and rationality. So it was not translated as the other classics were, and indeed no translation was available in a Western language until as late as 1834, when one appeared in Latin. Later came the great translations of James Legge and Richard Wilhelm that have so profoundly encouraged the West to take this great book to heart. In both cases the translators were in China because they were Christians. In both cases, they were unusual for Christians of their times because they did not hold the view that God had only revealed himself to the Jews and in the Bible; both saw

God at work in other cultures and at various times. Both of them regarded China as a country that equalled if not excelled any in the West, and as such they saw the Divine Hand at work in its history and development as much as in Israel and Christian Europe. In particular both Legge and Wilhelm moved in a bold group of Christians and free-thinkers who saw the Classics as the Chinese equivalent of the Pentateuch. In other words, they saw a Divine Witness that had become lost and obscured by folk and popular religion, just as they saw a Divine Message in the Old Testament that had become obscured by legalistic Judaism. For men such as this, translation was not carried out for academic interest but out of the conviction that here lay truth on a par with that of the Bible—and probably from the same Source. This led both men to employ certain terms and to make certain assumptions about what the book was saying and from whom it came. This certainly helped the West to accept it but it has not really helped the West to encounter the *I Ching* itself.

One of the main problems with Legge's and Wilhelm's translations is the arcane language used. Both versions sound like the Authorized Version on a bad day! But this is in fact part of the game. When they came to translate the book, Legge and Wilhelm deliberately made it sound as close to the most authorized translations of the Bible that they knew. In fact, Legge, an Englishman, made it sound like the Authorized Version itself, and Wilhelm, a German, made it sound like the Luther translation. The arcane quality of the style is meant to say to the perceptive reader, 'Here is the Chinese equivalent of our sacred revelation. Think on that and be amazed!'

Now, you may be wondering why I have taken you into the interesting but surely irrelevant world of translations. It is not irrelevant, however, for the message which Legge and Wilhelm saw in the *I Ching* has become the message that the West has given to the *I Ching*, albeit nowadays the Bible is as much a closed book to many as is Chinese culture!

What Legge and Wilhelm did, then, is tell us that the *I Ching* is speaking to us from a source that we already know, that its message is reassuringly familiar. In doing so, however, they actually misrepresented the fundamental *otherness* of the book and the fact that for the Chinese the messages, if such they be, do not come from some personal deity who lovingly seeks to guide our lives and who has revealed His will for humanity and all of life. Far from it. As a result, for most people the *I Ching* has been unable to deliver its most powerful message. It is therefore time to look at what the Chinese themselves believe about the book and about where its power and influence come from.

The first thing to appreciate is that the Chinese do not expect it to give them answers as such; rather, they turn to the *I Ching* to help them to make a decision. Too often in the West, however, people have tried to abdicate responsibility on to systems or forces beyond themselves which they feel or wish controlled their lives. Any such use of the *I Ching* is in fact a perversion of its power, meaning and radical challenge.

The Chinese use the *I Ching* to help clarify; to assist in decision-making; to guide but not to control; to offer a new perspective but not give a final answer. They also use it for meditation by the age-old method of simply opening the book at random, reading the first text that they come upon and then reflecting upon that for a while.

This actually gives us a clue to what the Chinese believe lies behind the *I Ching*. In Chinese thought, the world, existence itself, is controlled not by deities (though popular belief has a multitude of them) but by natural forces which have no divine power but which are the very power of the Universe. Within their ambit comes all life, including gods. The two basic forces, yin and yang, are opposites in the same way that day and night, male and female, hot and cold, and so forth are opposites. They are constantly struggling to excel over each other, yet they can never do so. However, the dynamic cause of this titanic, eternal but basically natural struggle is what keeps existence in perpetual motion. It is of course a motion that has various ups and downs, but these have a certain logic to them. The world is not static or meaningless; it is a world of *understandable change*.

Now, *I Ching* means 'Classic of Change'; it is about our place in a world, a cosmos that alters and fluctuates from moment to moment; a world in which we delude ourselves if we think we have a perfect system or method for understanding reality. So the *I Ching* is based on the assumption that nothing, not even the *I Ching* itself, can know what is happening or control it. This is why the use of the book in the West as a source of answers is so fundamentally misguided, for it is essentially a method for abandoning the attempt to rationalize, understand, control or determine the future. It asks us to use a totally random method for finding an apparently meaningless statement, and in so doing it breaks our attempt to reason and opens us up to the flow of natural forces. From this flows its wisdom.

To illustrate: the *I Ching* is not a book the Chinese believe you should use to find the winner of the 2.30 at Aintree tomorrow. Nor is it to find out the sex of an expected baby. There are plenty of other systems if that is what you want, though most good diviners would laugh at such expectations of any system. No, the *I Ching* is about indecision, ambiguity and uncertainty. For instance, if you have a choice to make about a job or whether to marry (not about *who* to marry but about marriage *per se*), then the *I Ching* can be helpful–revelatory, in fact. You know how it is. You have looked at this momentous choice from all angles. Some days you feel, 'Yes, it's right'; on other days you're just not sure. What is needed is a third voice which breaks into our rather pathetic attempts to rationalize about the future, to analyse what has yet to happen, to assess the inaccessible! This voice introduces an apparently unconnected factor into the equation. The result is often, though not always, fascinating. For this totally random factor can suddenly help clarify your thinking; can put things into a new light; can make you realize that what you want is not x or y but that you felt you had to justify wanting x and y. In the end the final decision is still left with you; the *I Ching* can never tell you what to do; but it can, so the Chinese believe, put you in touch, fleetingly but powerfully, with the change dimension in the Universe; it can break the arrogance of human reason and allow the pattern of the cosmic order to break into our remarkably feeble and petty minds for a moment, giving us a sense of what is significant and what is not. This is one of the most dramatic, powerful and potentially liberating forms of 'divination' possible, for it does not tell us but exposes us, and from this exposure we are left to make what we may of the experience, insight or whatever you wish to call it.

This is the power of the *I Ching*. This is why it has held centre stage for so long and so powerfully. And we in the West have barely grasped this, for the translations of Legge and Wilhelm were simply not concerned with revealing this fundamental outlook and could not do so for two very simple reasons: firstly, they had a different agenda: revealing a single God or source within both the Judaeo-Christian and Chinese cultures, and, secondly, because they used a Chinese text version and scholarship designed to obscure this power and make it serve a more venal task.

The text which both Legge and Wilhelm used was produced in 1715. It was a deliberate piece of political publishing in which the alien Mongol dynasty of Ch'ing sought to show the Chinese that the Ch'ing had the right to rule. In producing what was in effect a political *I Ching*, they deliberately turned their backs on the insights and commentaries of the most brilliant contemporary writers and students of the *I Ching* and instead chose time-servers and old texts. Many of these old texts are excellent, but the purpose to which they were put was less than inspirational! Not only this, but Wilhelm in particular, working in the 1920s, chose to do so with a displaced person, a man whose world had collapsed in

1911 when the empire fell and turned its republican back on the past. In other words, Wilhelm worked with a reactionary who had no place in modern China. As a result, he was fed a lot of extreme, reactionary, Ch'ing views on the *I Ching* and these have obscured the work ever since. For instance, when we told contemporary Chinese professional users of the *I Ching* about the moving lines, they were very amused. As they rightly pointed out, these have not been used for centuries in China and are irrelevant anyway. The beauty of the *I Ching* lies in its total randomness, and all this playing around with moving lines stems from the old human desire to try and reintroduce some measure of method, control and influence again. It is in fact an attempt to tame the wild energy of the *I Ching*.

This is why we at ICOREC[1] produced *The Contemporary I Ching*. Instead of rehashing the work of Legge, Wilhelm and their successors, which admittedly has been important in introducing the book to the Western consciousness, we turned to the contemporary users who came from the culture which gave birth to the book in the first place, to the unbroken line of Chinese users and commentators. With them we discovered the truly astonishing meaning of the *I Ching* and realized how the West, by asking its own questions first and then interpreting the answers to fit its own needs, had actually failed to allow the *I Ching* to speak to us in its own pure and raw way—a way which shatters many of our fondest illusions about who and what we are, how we 'run' the world and even think we understand it, and perhaps also threatens our understanding of who or what speaks to us through such a vehicle as the *I Ching*.

In the end, as always with the *I Ching*, it is left up to us to decide!

---

[1] International Consultancy of Religion, Education and Culture

Buddhism and Christianity—Bridging the Gap
John Crook

DURING ONE OF HIS VISITS TO EUROPE, H. H. the Dalai Lama stayed in a Christian monastery and was introduced to a monk who had just completed a long retreat. When asked about his practice, the monk had replied—the contemplation of love. His Holiness, impressed, remarked that this showed how close Christianity and Buddhism were to one another in their fundamental concerns and that a dialogue at that level would reveal common orientations to a religious life focused on compassion.

I want to make the case here for an increasing Buddhist-Christian dialogue in order that this common concern may receive deeper attention. It is important that men such as the Dalai Lama and Dr Runcie, the recent Archbishop of Canterbury, be heard and their intercourse with the powers of state given greater attention. Ultimately, world happiness depends on a compassionate concern for the optimization of material, spiritual and personal benefits for all. Certainly any philosophy focusing only on benefits for those of whom we approve will tend to be destructive, especially in an age in which concern for world society and global ecology is working poorly against the clock.

Christianity is of course no longer the prevailing world view of the people of Western civilization. Its monolithic status has crumbled before the rationalism and empiricism of the philosophies and sciences developed since the seventeenth century. We live today very much in a post-Christian world. Furthermore, in its attempts to retain a foothold in the contemporary scene, Christianity has given way before the needs of people for whom adolescence seems to be a permanent condition. To be young, monied, sexy, satisfied by emotive sensation and admired is the hedonistic blindness to which so many of us succumb. And our tendencies in that direction are reinforced continuously by the media which in turn reflect a common need. It is as if a major part of the Western world, created essentially by affluent consumerism, has suppressed its deeper needs for a meaningful existence and become stuck in a realm where sensation replaces insight; sensation, moreover, that can become addictive and a basis for drugged dependencies of many kinds. Churches with cut-back liturgies in which the subtle nuances of earlier form are lost, with sing-song jollification producing superficial togetherness and teachings of trite simplicity ignorant of any relation to the learning of our time, pander only to the simple minded who seek security outside themselves in imaginary heavenly powers.

Yet, against this pathetic background, 'deep' Christianity does still continue on its quieter way. In England, for example, tiny communities of Franciscan Anglicans lie hidden in the wooded recesses of rural regions and small monasteries of Catholic and Eastern Orthodox faith are still to be found. To visit them is an inspiration. It is this 'deep' Christianity which retains the qualities essential if a dialogue with Buddhism is to begin; for only here is there a sufficient seriousness and intellectual commitment to meet the challenge of a rapidly spreading appreciation of Buddhist philosophy and practice among thinking Westerners.

THE PHILOSOPHICAL AND CONCEPTUAL SEPARATION

In spite of the important level of common concern, Buddhism and Christianity do none the less remain conceptually in different worlds. Their interpretations of the meaning of human existence differ in certain fundamental ways. For dialogue to occur there will have to be a willingness on both sides to subject all statements of faith to radical critical analysis. This is vital, for deep theodicy requires deconstruction. Theodical assertions are merely such, yet at a level behind or below them are more vital ontological, ethical and soteriological positions wherein overlaps of interest appear. Powerful statements such as the Beatitudes or the Four Noble Truths are highly coded texts that need sensitive hermeneutic examination in awareness of the times in which they were formulated and of the way in which they may be relevant today.

I. HISTORICISM

The Christian claim for an especial relevance of the person of Jesus Christ in the interpretation of history is often regarded as fundamental. As the Son of God sent as a redeemer for human sin, the person of Christ was rooted in divine time and, indeed, we date our years from that moment. This traditional perspective was, furthermore, developed from the older Judaic notion of an especial relationship between Jehovah and Israel. In both cases there was a tight link between the Almighty and a chosen people. Yet, as Peter Berger (1967) has shown, this single link became vulnerable as soon as its credibility was called in question and, as the Renaissance gathered strength, alternative world views became available. The quasi-religions, as Tillich (1963) called them, Scientism, Marxism, the nihilism of Nietzsche, and reductionist psychology including psychoanalysis, all draw their strength from a focus on the power of a precisely human ingenuity to change the world and the course of history. As Masao Abe stresses (1985) these systems comprise a secularism that may provide important roots for meaningful action, an alternative for religious aspiration, but which can also sometimes become negatively anti-religious. Values for action are then based solely on intellectualized interpretations of human nature that are dogmatic in tone and do not allow as relevant any expression of reason based on the heart. The world already made subject to humanity within Christianity becomes a potential victim of man's designs. It is no longer the sacred; and what was thought to be sacred has been called in question.

Buddhism, by contrast, does not make much of an issue out of the historicity of Gautama the Buddha. His teachings did not include assertions about the nature of any transcending power. They focused instead upon certain processes which, known to us by reason of their expression in the mind, are also considered basic to our relationship with the Universe as a whole. There is no hot line to a deity here. The Universe appears within a felt sacredness which is immediately and naturally present before the distorting gaze of our ignorance. In Buddhism a profound monism stands contrasted with the dualism inherent in Christian historicism.

II. THE PROBLEM OF GOD

As modern physics reveals the enormity of cosmic space and the riddle it poses for any ultimate explanation, so the attention of Western thinkers has turned to an examination of the way in which we conceive and utilize our models of the world. Science can say nothing of what is beyond its reach. Faced with the impossibility of verifying any ultimate assertion, some theologians have adopted a 'death of God' perspective in which they have sought for a Christianity which could do without a transcendent concept. Yet this attempt only reflects the impasse that has emerged within Western philosophy itself.

As thinkers such as Heidegger, Wittgenstein and Derrida have pointed out, the entire quest of Western philosophy since the Greeks has been bound up with attempts to invoke or preserve the transcendental. The collapse of this enduring effort, as Don Cupitt (1987) has eloquently shown, takes Christianity with it in so far as Christianity has been dependent on these conceptions. Floating in the void so created, Christians like Cupitt seek relevance for their faith in a form of biocultural humanism in which religious texts are seen to inform us of ways of being which, as in Christ, may become incarnate and with which we may 'resonate' meaningfully.

This then is a contemporary Christianity made of 'fleshwords' (loc. cit. p.166) that seek to 'awaken the creative-desire-flow of the religious life' they describe. Christ, like us, was human; in the word and flesh of Christ we can find a mirror to ourselves and our potential. There is an acceptance of contemporary sociobiology here with which Darwin would not quarrel and a genuine attempt to get beyond the dualism of the traditional dogmas. Within such a perspective it is the imitation of Christ rather than a relationship with God that moves to the forefront. In accepting Cartesian science and linguistic philosophy as an intellectual basis, we remain in an abyss of meaninglessness with respect to the Universe as a whole.

At first sight Buddhism relates to science, especially psychology (Crook 1980, Crook and Rabgyas 1988), in a not dissimilar manner. Indeed Cupitt's references to Zen suggest an awareness of this. Yet, although lacking in assertions about the ultimate, Buddhism shows how, in relating to the proximate, sacred value can be conserved through a profound appreciation of both the depths and the limitations of mind.

Basic to Zen psychology, for example, is a tradition which envisages a 'storehouse' consciousness—a 'womb of suchness' in which experience and the experienced merge in one continuum. When the mind focuses on any particular detail, that detail is isolated as a conceptual reification. Although such a process is deemed essential for relating conventionally to the world, it is in essence illusory. As in the contemporary cognitive psychology of the West, the mind operates with representations of the 'real' which can never be more than models. If the mind goes in quest of the modeller, it eventually reaches a state in which it stares straight into the mental space from which thought comes and finds 'nothing'—except the world in its immediate apprehension.

This 'freedom from the known', as Krishnamurti calls it, is felt as a liberation giving rise to bliss and maybe love. Names of this state, being only names, come coated with potential illusion and open to egoic intrusion. They include terms like the 'Unborn Mind'. Is it conceivable that this pre-intellectual relationship with thoughtless experience could also be called 'God'? If so, the term would have meaning only in the context of immanence, for what is transcended here is merely the occupation of the mind by thought. Yet, if this is an adequate and 'true' account of mystical experience, and if such experience is all the evidence we have for 'God', perhaps this is as far as we can go.

Gautama had gone in search of divinity within the Brahminical view of his time. A major contribution to his enlightenment was the realization that all that could be discovered within experience was the interdependence of the processes that together sustain appearance. In Buddhism, the transcendent is none other than the immanent. Furthermore, within immanence no appearance can be found to have a separable distinctive selfhood as an entity; everything is in a mutually relating movement. The Indian philosopher Nagarjuna, anticipating modern linguistic philosophy by nearly 2,000 years, applied the same principle to the subtle interdependence of words. Whether in words or 'reality', everything reduces to the one—and to what does the one reduce remains a paradoxical question, a subject for meditational voyaging.

Within 'deep' Christianity there is a tradition sympathetic to such a view. The apophatic vision of God found in the collection of writing by the early Fathers known as the 'Love of the Good' (*Philokalia*—see Kadloubovski and Palmer 1957), the Athonite tradition (see Meyendorff 1964), and writings of Pseudo-Dionysian flavour such as the sermons of Eckhart (Walshe 1979) or the *Cloud of Unknowing* (Wolters 1961), all have vibrations that can engage the Buddhist vision. The dialogue that interests us can in fact proceed much more easily on a basis of the *via negativa* of the Eastern churches than on the more categorical assertions of the Western ones. There are parallels here that invite conjoint exploration, as do re-examinations of the solitary and contemplative life within Christianity as a whole (Allchin 1977).

III. SOTERIOLOGICAL CONCERNS

The paths to salvation in traditional Christianity and Buddhism differ in ways that hinge on the key concepts of sin and karma. Sins entail guilt or shame and necessitate forgiveness. The story of the Fall in Genesis represents the origin of sin in a vivid analogy. Christianity indeed is perhaps first and foremost a religion of forgiveness and its conception of compassion rests within this frame. The figure of the Redeemer has enormous archetypical power, stemming from the need most of us feel for some sort of redemption. Inappropriate desire, pride, deceit and lack of love are the consequences of many human conditions and need to be transcended. The belief in the Redeemer lifts the burden from one who feels powerless and hopeless and restores a primal innocence. Wilful crime leads to hell, and Christianity has not failed to terrorize its adherents into morality by providing visions of a hellish destination for sinners—nicely graded to suit the sin.

Buddhism has its hells too but since beings migrate through many lives sojourn there is not permanent. For the Buddhist, painful consequences stem from evil intentions, but these can be atoned for through repentance and willed action towards the good. A happy life is the result of good actions. An individual is therefore always in charge of his or her destiny and can 'work out salvation with diligence'. There is no other authority out there as judge—the process does its work as the expression of its nature.

It is clear then that the basis of moral life is very differently conceived in Christianity and in Buddhism. It could almost be said that in the first book of the Bible God sets man up for the Fall by giving him the awareness of choice. Man's failure to choose wisely is the endless disgrace from which he is incapable of recovery without a redemption ordained through God by virtue of the mission of his Son. The complex relations between choice, sin, the Fall and redemption define human moral attributes in a very precisely codified way. There is a human powerlessness here, for, in crucifying Christ, man fell a second time, even though the hope of redemption, once given, was not taken away. Forgiveness in the end can only come from God. Man alone is irredeemable.

The Buddhist is not burdened in this way. Yet, for him/her too, choice is the key element in moral life and the Precepts are a guide to a correct view ensuring a way that can reduce and may eliminate the self-doubt and misery consequent upon desire for permanent being. It is indeed the insight into impermanence and the illusion of egoism that gives rise to clear comprehension and a realization that in delivering others from misery one also delivers oneself. The emphasis here is on a process in which one can participate or, to one's cost, ignore.

The origins of these contrasting beliefs must lie in the social histories that determined their conceptual evolution. An analysis in such terms would reveal their essential relativity and cast a light on how we may perhaps reconceive them in our own times.

IV. PATHS OF CONVERGENCE

It is no accident that at the same time as a larger proportion of humanity than ever before has 'never had it so good' in terms of personal comfort, wealth and mobility, so ecological destruction arising from economic activity wreaks havoc on the global environment at an ever increasing pace. Those in power are not blind to what is happening but seemingly do not care sufficiently to tackle historical constraints and vested interests in a manner consistent enough to stave off disaster. At a time when an optimism on the political front gains ground and the nuclear threat recedes, so hidden ecological and demographic themes move ever more menacingly from the shadows.

The major world religions have a responsibility for this situation. In particular, the Christian failure to regard the natural world as sacred has permitted economic exploitation of world resources without sensitive restraint. Biological awareness rather than any system of ethics has sounded the alarm. The rising tide of hedonistic secular utilitarianism drives a technological civilization requiring energy taken from limited global resources and which emits polluting waste in ways impossible in earlier times (Boyden 1989). Faced with problems on a wholly new dimension, Western society currently has no guiding light in a philosophical orientation to the Universe which technologically it knows so well. Those humanistic themes which do include an environmental theme are derived basically from older Christian principles and they too lack any fundamental view.

What, then, would a fundamental view be? It must surely be some stance towards the unknown that is heartfelt and includes an acceptance of human capacity and limitation. By 'heartfelt' I mean a view that engages feeling at a level where there is a sense of involvement with fate and not merely an intellectually constructed utopianism. Such a stance requires an honesty which rejects mere wishful thinking, faces up to the limits of human knowledge, focuses upon ways in which our technical know-how can best be applied and is devoted to an optimization of economic action rather than a run-away maximization of gain.

This planet is now over-run by human beings much as a house may be infested by rats. It will require a willed intelligence to improve our damaged living rooms. And, since human beings are sensitive to beauty, these rooms need to conserve the natural wonders of the planet for these comprised the natural environment of our evolutionary origin from which our awareness of beauty itself stemmed. Otherwise there is real possibility that we may hand on to succeeding generations merely a wrecked basement filled with the ordures of excess. To achieve such intelligence we have to rediscover a sense of the sacred.

Although Wittgenstein (1953) counselled us to look for the use of conceptual models rather than for their meaning, the quest for meaning seems to be bred into our system of intellectual enquiry. Meaning can, however, take many forms, for it is essentially an attribution arising from a confluence of understandings. In attributing meaning to human life today we cannot ignore the relativity of our knowledge, the destructiveness of our behaviour and the meanness of our ethics. We have to take on the burning situation of our present time. This is a responsibility which the shame of the great religions imposes upon us.

We began by speaking of compassion. Christian compassion has tended to focus on poverty. It is an action-man religion in which missionary efforts are often aided through benefiting the poor. More generously put, Christianity has seriously concerned itself with misery. Today it focuses especially not so much on economic distress but upon the misery of the bourgeoisie. As it spreads, this misery, the predominant social malaise of our time, spawns hopeful psychotherapies: some soundly based on Western or Eastern psychology, some merely cranky. One place for convergence then would be for Christians to learn the Buddhist approach to the relief of misery and for Buddhists to concern themselves more with social action (see Brandon 1976, Jones 1989, Abe 1985).

The Buddhist approach to misery is rooted in its view of the nature of mind. Is it possible for Christians to 'buy' that view and yet remain true to themselves? One route would be to bring forward the apophatic view of God—the *via negativa*. This would allow individuals in contemplative prayer to experience 'God' in the immanence of life without the confusion occasioned by those transcendental concepts that are now linked with disbelief. Indeed, a method of doing this is already available in the medieval text, *The Cloud of Unknowing*, in which an unknown spiritual adviser counsels a young priest to go in quest of God without any preconceptions of what the experience of meeting might be like.

'Imagine yourself seated in a great cloud on the summit of a mountain,' he says. 'As each and every concept of God arises, chuck it out into the Cloud of Forgetting below you. Keep gazing into the Cloud of Unknowing before you. After many hours you will come to the end of concepts. Then the Cloud will part and you will see.' Such an exercise differs little from work on a Zen koan or paradoxical question: one that cannot be answered but only resolved in the appreciation of paradox. 'What is God?' is indeed such a question. Christians such as Merton (1977) and Johnston (1971) have already discovered the value of such a route. With greater clarity achieved in this way, it would then be possible to move on to a koan closer to the concerns of Don Cupitt. Such a koan would be 'Tell me what the Cross is?' As the meditator in zazen merged with this question he may well gain a profound insight into the meaning of his faith. This may be uncanonical or even idiosyncratic but it would have the power of personal revelation. It would not be difficult for a person trained in the running of Zen retreats and aware of the Christian problematique to establish a context in which such work could be done. The implication in terms of a rediscovery of heartfelt meaning could be considerable. Furthermore, a Christian could then widen his sense of the sacred by asking in zazen, 'Who are sentient beings?': a question inevitably leading to the environmental issue.

Another path whereby a Christian approach to misery could be enhanced would be through the use of visualization. I have often been surprised at the limited psychological use to which the Eastern churches put their revered ikons. In many ways ikons resemble Tibetan thangkas. The latter are, however, the basis for profound inner journeys or transformations in which the meditator creates in his own being that of the Buddha (say) on the painting. Now, it is important to note that the lamas are against any superstition here. The texts usually include comments indicating that this is purely a work of visualization; no real objective Buddha has done anything. None the less the practice makes the mind closer to that of a Buddha. As part of a system of self-transformation the method is a powerful one. Here is certainly a method that awakens 'the creative-desire-flow of the religious life it describes' (Cupitt loc. cit.).

Buddhists have not been notably successful at social action. The loss of Tibet is a dramatic case in point. Yet in Vietnam and now also in the West there is a sense that it is important ro re-enter 'the market place with helping hands' (Kapleau 1965, p.311). While Buddhists will always need to train in retreat and to discover themselves in solitude, too great an application here would smack of the defect of the arhat—one said to seek salvation merely for him/herself. The bodhisattva of the Mahayana may be said to be one who 'alone with others' (Batchelor 1983) concerns him/herself in modern times with practical works with and for other people in a full understanding of the culture in which we now live.

<h2 style="text-align:center">CONCLUSION</h2>

It has not been my intention to suggest that some sort of *mélange* of Christian and Buddhist beliefs would be desirable as a response to our times. Rather it has seemed to me important that these two highly developed and socially significant systems of belief should get to know one another and share common concerns and differences. Already small groups of Christian monks and intellectuals have visited the reconstituted Tibetan monastic universities in India and found value in dialogue. In many ways both systems seek the common good and have that heartfelt quality that secular endeavours lack. The psychological depth of religion has been neglected to our cost and, in our need for a rediscovery of values, such a dialogue is likely to be of benefit to all.

The common concern with compassion provides a basis for Christian-Buddhist dialogue. Compassion, however, needs to be comprehended within a universal vision. It is not only with a feeling of kindness for human beings and other sentient creatures that we are concerned. If 'letting others be' is a prime rule in the practice with regards fellow humans, so too it may be given a wider environmental meaning. Compassion for landscape, for the myriad organisms of a forest, for the rocks, stones and trees that are the natural expression of our planet, is also a cardinal, yet neglected, principle (Ash 1987). Neglect it and we commit hubris—as the pre-Christian Greeks in their myth of Prometheus so well understood. And hubris, like karma, has inevitable consequences all too apparent in our present world. Without compassion for the earth, the animals and the plants, we slowly kill ourselves even as we bring about the death of a living planet. Perhaps in the immense and turning aeons of time this is the way things have been before and maybe will be again. Does the evolution of life necessarily entail a selfishness that in the end destroys itself? Yet we do have a choice as to the outcome—now and only now. It begins in a heart that can envision itself situated within a sacredness that ultimately cannot be described—except in terms of selfless love.

REFERENCES
Abe, M. 1985. *Zen and Western Thought*. London, Macmillan.
Allchin, A.M. 1977. *Solitude and Communion: Papers on the Hermit Life*. Oxford, SLG Press.
Ash, M. 1987. *New Renaissance: essays in search of wholeness*. Hartland, Devon, Green Books.
Batchelor, S. 1983. *Alone with Others*. New York, Grove Press.
Berger, P. 1967. *The Social Reality of Religion*. London, Penguin.
Boyden, S. 1989. *Western Civilization in Biological Perspective*. Oxford University Press.
Brandon, D. 1976. *Zen in the Art of Helping*. London, Routledge and Kegan Paul.
Crook, J.H. 1980. *The Evolution of Human Consciousness*. Oxford University Press.
Crook, J.H. and Tashi Rabgyas. 1988. 'The Essential Insight: a central theme in the philosophical training of Mahayanist monks.' In: Paranjpe, A.C, Ho, D.Y. and Rieber, E. *Asian Contributions to Psychology*. New York, Praeger.

Cupitt, D. 1987. *The Long Legged Fly: A Theology of Language and Desire*. London, SCM.

Johnston, W. 1971. *Christian Zen*. New York, Harper Colophon.

Jones, K. 1989. *The Social Face of Buddhism*. London, Wisdom Publications.

Kadloubovsky, E. and Palmer, G.E.H. 1957. *Writings from the Philokalia on Prayer of the Heart*. London, Faber and Faber.

Kapleau, P. *The Three Pillars of Zen*. New York, Beacon.

Kasulis, T.P. 1981. *Zen Action, Zen Person*. University Press of Hawaii.

Meyendorff J. 1964. *A Study of Gregory Palamas*. Leighton Buzzard, The Faith Press.

Merton, T. 1977. *The Monastic Journey*. London, Sheldon Press.

Tillich, P. 1963. *Christianity and the Encounter of World Religions*. New York, Columbia University Press.

Walshe, M.O'C. 1979. *Meister Eckhart, Sermons and Treatises*. Shaftesbury, Element Books.

Wittgenstein, L. 1953. *Philosophical Investigations*. Oxford, Blackwell.

Wolters, C. (Trans). 1961. *The Cloud of Unknowing*. London, Penguin Books.

Spiritual Dimensions of Islam
Gai Eaton

WE HAVE TO START with a definition of Sufism and that always seems very easy. We say, 'Sufism is the mystical dimension of Islam.' Fine, then everybody thinks they know what it is about and that's that. Unfortunately, it is more complicated, and it might startle you if I say that the vast majority of Sufis are not mystics and they have no pretension to be mystics, and there are moreover many Muslims who, I think, would be qualified as mystics but are not Sufis.

Now, to explain the first point: why most Sufis are not mystics. Islam is a very disorganized religion and that, like most things in this world, has its advantages and its disadvantages. If you wonder what the advantages of being disorganized are, well let me give you one example. The Chinese Communists in their determination to wipe out religion found it fairly easy to deal with Christianity because there were specific heads that could be bashed or cut off. They were extremely puzzled when it came to dealing with the Muslims of China, however, because they couldn't locate any specific leader or official power and so they couldn't find the right person to execute or imprison. Of course, in practice every Muslim is in a very real sense self-sufficient before God. On the other hand, many of the troubles that we have in the world of Islam today turn upon lack of order and in times of difficulty and danger people need some sort of leadership and organization.

Now, this is a gap in the whole structure of Islam which has been filled by the Sufi brotherhoods, which we call the *tariquahs*.

These exist in a series of concentric circles. At the centre is the *shaikh*. Around him will range a number of disciples, who probably spend most of their time with him and will certainly be qualified either as mystics or as people who aspire to mystical knowledge and mystical states. There is then a further, looser circle of people, perhaps very busy in their lives as farmers or what have you, but who nonetheless spend what time they can visiting the *shaikh*, coming to *tariquah* meetings and, in rather a modest way, trying to follow a mystical path.

Beyond these there is yet another group, often very simple peasants who don't have much free time and who may visit their *shaikh* two or three times in their lives, ask him a few simple questions perhaps about personal problems, receive simple answers, but who say proudly to their friends and neighbours, 'I am a discipline of Shaikh so-and-so.' They go also for the *barakah*. We usually translate *barakah* as grace, but the Christian idea of grace doesn't fully embrace it. *Barakah* is a quality which adheres to the sacred, to saints and, as far as most Sufis are concerned, to the graves of saints. The simple people who visit a saintly man believe that just by sitting at his feet or listening to him they have absorbed a kind of spiritual influence, which is a mixture of spiritual influence in the highest sense and good luck. Simple people have always confused these two and I'm not sure that they are wrong.

Even beyond that circle, if it is a time of war or danger or difficulty, there will be a whole lot of other people who will attach themselves to the *tariquah* simply as a refuge. Bennigsen, the great authority on the Muslims of the Soviet Union, has written that one-third of the population of the northern Caucusus belong to Sufi brotherhoods. I don't know anything about the people of the northern Caucusus, but I very much doubt whether one third of the population are mystics in that sense. The point is that, under the oppression of a militant atheist regime, a Sufi *tariquah* offers some degree of organization, leadership and indeed a certain measure of worldly security in that it often acts as a welfare organization for poor members of the group.

Now, just as there are Sufis who are in no sense mystics, there are also non-Sufi Muslims who might be called mystics. The ordinary practices of Islam—the Five Daily Prayers, the example of the Prophet and his night vigils, the Ramadan fast and the requirement to remember God much and often—are already the basis for a mystical life. Therefore those who perhaps, for one reason or another, disapprove of Sufism (as many Muslims do) may nonetheless be men or women of such piety that I think the word 'mystic' could reasonably be applied to them.

So how do we distinguish between the two?

What really characterizes a member of a Sufi *tariquah* is first the *bay'ah*, the oath of allegiance which he makes to his *shaikh* simply by taking his hand and the *shaikh* then pronouncing certain formulae from the Koran. This is in imitation of an occasion when the Companions, in a time of great danger, came to Muhammad and renewed their *bay'ah* (oath) to him. Secondly, there is the *silsilah*, literally the chain: the lineage of spiritual descent that is grafted onto our human nature when we come to a Sufi *tariquah*. Every member of a *tariquah* will have the tree of his spiritual ancestry. At the top will be the name of God, Allah; below that comes the Angel Gabriel, the Angel of Revelation; then comes Muhammad; then the name of probably Ali or Abu Bakr, one of the Prophet's closest Companions; under that, the name of someone to whom he passed on the spiritual influence; and then you will have perhaps some thirty names, recorded usually with the date of their death, which connect you as a member of the *tariquah* today in 1989 with that whole chain.

I am now going to have to go into a bit of history, because there are so many misunderstandings about Sufism, and not only amongst non-Muslims, that it is impossible to put you in the picture without doing so. The revelation of Muhammad starts as a synthesis containing all possibilities that may be fulfilled by human beings, both spiritually or in action—if you like, almost a germ as yet undeveloped. The early community in Medina, the city of the Prophet, was undoubtedly a community of such extraordinary piety, devotion to the faith and sincerity that it is difficult to say where the borderline between spirituality or mysticism, on the one hand, and action, on the other, can be drawn. However, only twenty-eight years after the death of the Prophet the last of what we call the Rightly-Guided Alis, was assassinated. He had been one of the four closest Companions of the Prophet, who later became the leaders of the community. When the last one died, leadership of the community was taken over by a man whose name is still, after all this time, cursed by many Muslims and who has been described by European historians as the Islamic Caesar. His name was Mu'awiyah.

Now the point about this man was, first, that he was the son of the Prophet's greatest enemy, Abu Sufyan, who had led the pagans repeatedly in war against the Muslims and had done everything in his power to destroy Muhammad and the newborn religion. There is no reason to suppose that Mu'awiyah, his son, was an insincere Muslim but he was a man of action: a conqueror rather than a spiritual man. When he gained (some say, usurped) power over the community he was already Governor of Syria with his seat at Damascus. Therefore, the seat of power moved from Medina, the city of the Prophet, to Damascus, the city of worldly power and grandeur. To my mind, that is where one sees the beginning of a division in Islam between spiritual men and the men of action. For, immediately after Mu'awiyah took power, the great conquests began which, within a hundred years of Muhammad's death, had brought Muslim armies not only to the borders of China but into Southern France.

Most people know about the great Muslim civilization of Spain, but many do not realize that the Muslims were in southern France and southern Switzerland for some two hundred years. This in itself was a very dubious exercise. The Koran is quite specific: you fight in self-defence or because you or your family have been driven unjustly from your home. So how on earth did these Muslim armies feel justified in going out and conquering most of the known world? It wasn't to convert people. At that time the Arabs felt that to be Muslim was such a privilege that they didn't really want other people to embrace Islam.

What happened I think was this. Umar, the third Caliph, who had been a Companion of the Prophet, was very anxious to prevent expansion, but the soldiers then were what they will always be: they liked to practice their job and to do so success-fully. There is a famous story about how one particular general, who had once fought against Islam but had been converted and was now leading the Muslim army, conquered Palestine and eventually reached the borders of Egypt. There he received an official sealed letter from Umar, but being a canny man and guessing what might be in it, he quietly stepped across the agreed frontier between the two countries. He then opened the letter, which said, 'If you have not yet crossed into Egypt, you must go no further. If you are already in Egypt you may proceed.' The general then looked around and asked, 'Are we by any chance in Egypt now?' 'Yes, sir, we are'—and on they went.

There is another reason for the Muslim conquests: Islam appeared at a time when the world was in a most extraordinary mess. Quite how many Christian sects there were nobody knows, but certainly well over two hundred, and they were all more or less fighting each other. The gates of Jerusalem were actually thrown open to the Muslims by the Patriarch, because he thought that rule by Muslims would be preferable to rule by fellow Christians of a different denomination.

And, of course, if you are leading a euphoric, triumphant band of people fired by a new religion and the thrill of discovery, and if there is virtually no resistance to you, the next mile tempts you another mile and so you go on and on . . . This, I think, is how it really happened, because it is a curious business that a religion which has very strict rules governing when you might or might not fight should in fact have conquered most of the known world.

Now, it's difficult to say when the word 'Sufi', which is associated simply with the wearing of simple woollen clothes, actually arose, but with hindsight the first Sufi is considered to have been Hasan al-Basri (642-728 CE). Like those early Desert Fathers in Christianity, he was an extreme ascetic, which is rather against the tenets of Islam insofar as it is a religion of moderation and does not favour extreme forms of self-denial.

Here we come to something which I think is worth mentioning in a short digression. We tend to say that religion has three aspects or can be practised in three different ways: a way of action (or fear), a way of love and a way of knowledge. Those of you who are acquainted with Hindu Vedanta will at once know what I am talking about. Now, of course, so far as the three religions descended from Abraham are concerned, we tend to say that this is exemplified first by Judaism as a religion of fear of the Lord, the religion of action, second by Christianity as the religion of love, and third by Islam as the religion of knowledge. We also say that the same pattern repeats itself within a religion and therefore, in that first Sufi, Hasan al-Basri, you see a demonstration of the way of fear, the way of action: all that mattered was to find forgiveness for his own unworthiness, to escape from the hellfire which he was sure he deserved. And yet within a very short time we have one of the most extraordinary mystics of divine love the world has known. That is Rabi'ah al-Adawiyah (d.801 CE). She started life as a slave girl, was freed very early on by her master who clearly saw what was in her and would have been very afraid to retain his rights as master over her. Hers was the religion of pure devoted love of God. She was reproached often enough for not marrying, because those who do not marry tend to be regarded with certain suspicion in Islam, but being a woman of some wit she said:

'I would gladly marry if I could meet a real man but in the whole of Baghdad I know one who is half a man, but I know no real man so I'm not going to get married.'

She liked to drive her points home in rather a graphic manner and on one occasion she was seen strolling through the streets of Baghdad with a burning brand in one hand and a pail of water in the other.

Not unnaturally, someone said, 'Rabi'ah, what on earth do you think you are doing?'

'I'm taking this brand to burn down Paradise so that nobody will worship God out of desire for Paradise, they will worship God only for himself alone,' she replied. 'I'm taking this water to drown out hell so that nobody will worship God for fear of hell but only from true and sincere love of God.'

It's a very typical Islamic image and it is very typical of Rabi'ah, who of course has had some publicity in the West. There have been a number of books about her, because clearly a woman of that eminence and of that period is of considerable interest.

Soon after Rabi'ah died, by the middle of the ninth century, things were changing in Islam. Millions and millions of new converts were coming in and they needed to be told what to do and what not to do. You know the old Victorian story: 'Go and see what little Johnnie is doing and tell him not to.' This, I think, was probably the spirit of many of the Muslim legalists and jurists at that time. Previously, the principles had been quite simply that you follow the Koran and above all you follow the *Sunna*, the example of the Prophet. But the example of the Prophet is contained in the many volumes of his sayings and his doings, many of which necessarily contradict each other because he might have said one thing to someone according to their need and another to someone else in other circumstances. But there it was, and to some extent you could choose what you did.

In the ninth century the four great schools of law were developed. There was not very much difference between them except in the most trivial sort of things: how, for example, you hold your hands in the ritual prayer and how strictly you have to observe certain practices. Anyway, a very, very rigid structure was suddenly arising—and of course rigidity is not always welcome to everybody but above all it tends to provoke a reaction. This reaction was a great development in the strengthening of Sufism. But it was a dangerous time: Mansur al-Hallaj (857-922 CE) spent eight years in jail for heresy and was finally cruelly executed.

Now, already there was an outward division in Sufism between what are called the 'sober' mystics and the 'drunken' ones, though there is no difference inwardly. The 'sober' mystic keeps his counsel; he is careful not to shock simple, ordinary people who might be confused by mystical ideas and he is discreet. The 'drunken' mystic, on the other hand, is the one who cannot resist shouting the mysteries of the Godhead from the rooftops. Al-Hallaj was the archetypal 'drunken' mystic. His principal offence, although there are many other things he said which attracted the wrath of the legalists, was his famous 'Ana al-Haqq!'—'I am the divine Truth!' in effect, 'I am God.' Of course he didn't mean, 'I, this miserable little ego, is God.' He meant, 'I have so emptied this person of my ego, I have so annihilated myself, that there is room for God here and God speaks and God says, "Ana al-Haqq. I am the Truth." It is nothing to do with me: He says it through me.' But, of course, that kind of argument was hardly likely to find favour with people who had no idea what he was talking about. He was scourged and he was crucified. This is why I think Christians have been so fascinated by him, because he knew what he was doing and he knew what was coming to him and therefore there was always a comparison with Jesus: the example of a sacrificial destiny faced and accepted. Because it was very un-Islamic to execute anybody for heresy (in fact, there were certain political undercurrents involved), the death of al-Hallaj shocked the Muslim community.

Very soon afterwards an extra-ordinary man arose, al-Ghazali (1058-1111CE), who produced the necessary reconciliation between the rigid legalists and the mystics. Al-Ghazali started out as a doctor of law who had no equal in his understanding. Losing his faith, he then went into seclusion for a long period. He travelled; he questioned the representatives of many different schools and sects. Only amongst the Sufis did he find satisfaction. Eventually he came back to a professorial chair in Baghdad with double authority. Nobody could challenge al-Ghazali for nobody knew more of the law then he did; and yet he was, in the fullest possible sense, one of the greatest mystics that the world has seen, but a sober mystic. In the greatest of his works, *The Rediscovery (or the Revival) of Knowledge*, he speaks of every possible aspect of life: of the highest reaches of mysticism, but also of the rules for washing yourself before you pray and the positions in prayer and so on.

In about a hundred years the greatest of them all was born in Andalusia: Ibn'Arabi (1163-1240CE). Those interested in Meister Eckhart will already have a clue to Ibn'Arabi, for although Eckhart was born just about the year Ibn'Arabi died, their similarity is quite extraordinary. Now, Ibn'Arabi gradually travelled from his birth place in Spain throughout the world of Islam, gathering people around him whenever he went. His influence on Sufism for the next four centuries at least, if not five, was so great that you could scarcely say there was any Sufism outside the Akbarist view (Ibn'Arabi is refered to by many people as *al-Shaikh al-Akbar*, the Greatest of Masters). I can't say very much about him in the limited time I have at my disposal, but, like Eckhart, he has something important to say to the modern age, which is the age of questioning, the age when simple unquestioning faith becomes more and more difficult. This quotation from a book by Fritjof Schuon has a close bearing on this:

It must be admitted that the progressives are not entirely wrong in thinking that there is something in religion which no longer works. In fact, the individualistic and sentimental argumentation with which traditional piety operates has lost almost all its power to pierce consciences and the reason for this is not merely that modern man is irreligious but also that the usual religious arguments, through not probing sufficiently to the depths of things and not having had previously any need to do so, are psychologically somewhat outworn and fail to satisfy certain needs of causality. If human societies degenerate on the one hand with the passage of time, they accumulate on the other experience by virtue of old age, however intermingled with errors their experience may be. This paradox is something that any pastoral teaching bent on efficacy should take into account, not by drawing new directives from the general error but, on the contrary, using arguments of a higher order.

Now, I've had people say to me, 'Your approach is very intellectual.' Well, fine for those who are happy with a religious faith which has no intellectual dimension at all. God bless them; they are amongst the salt of the earth; but in the modern world they are in constant danger. Take, let us say, some simple Italian peasant whose Catholic faith is absolutely unquenchable; his son is bright and goes to university and learns to be questioning and comes home to Daddy and says, 'Why do you believe this and that. Surely that's just superstition?'; and Daddy can't answer and his own faith begins to be in difficulty. This applies very much in Islam. Now what Ibn'Arabi and Eckhart do is to produce arguments and ideas which are not particularly easy but are there to satisfy those who insist upon asking certain questions and who have the application.

There are two things in Ibn'Arabi that I think are particularly useful. One is his statement that when, after death, we all stand (as we must) before God, believers will first see God in the form in which they expected to see him; and then this form will change into the form of God understood by another faith and these believers will be very puzzled indeed; and then the form of God will change yet again into the form in which He is known in another faith and in awful confusion those believers will suddenly find that their image of God is not the only one. Now, what Ibn'Arabi is not afraid to say is that our idea of God, whether we be Christians, Muslim or what have you, is a projection. Of course, atheists and agnostics also say that God is a projection of the unconscious, of wishful think-ing and so on. But what Ibn'Arabi was saying was this is a projection willed by God in his mercy as a means of communi-cation, because man as man cannot communicate with the divine essence, the Godhead, as such. Therefore, there has to be a God who is indeed in our own image, an anthropomorphic God, even if that is not the ultimate Reality. Nonetheless, for Ibn'Arabi Reality accepts our devotion, our worship, channelled through this idea. This notion provides a basis for, if you like, modern ecumenism.

There is another very important doctrine which was not spe-cific to Ibn'Arabi: the doctrine of the Five Divine Presences or *Hadarat*. What he meant was five degrees of reality, five orders of reality. You could say five hundred or five million of course, because they are infinite, but we like to have concepts simplified as an aid to understanding.

The Fifth Hadrah is the material world. It is very, very fragile. If God were to turn his eye away for one moment it would disappear in a puff of smoke. Nonetheless, it is the apparent form of Reality that we do see and touch around us. This is enveloped and encompassed in the Fourth Hadrah: the psy-chic domain, which Ibn'Arabi regards as still part of nature, thereby immediately wiping out any idea that ghosts, spirits and what have you are supernatural. They simply belong to an unseen dimension that penetrates the material as a sponge is penetrated by water. Above that, the Third Hadrah, infinitely more vast and penetrating, is what could be called the angelic domain. In a way it is the domain of commerce between Nature and God and therefore of the angels. The Fourth Hadrah is that of the personal God whom we do not understand but who we can worship, love and speak to in prayer. Beyond, infinitely beyond the personal God, the ultimate reality is what Eckhart called the Godhead and in Islam is called the Divine Essence, of which nothing can be said, for to do so would be to limit it. Similarly in Hindu Vedanta it is preferable to call ultimate Reality non-dual rather than a unity because unity is already a definition, whereas 'non-dual' avoids definition. But everything that is or could be, everything imaginable on every possible level of reality, is nonetheless contained in the absolute silence of the Divine Essence, which is both total darkness and total light.

About two hundred years ago, when Islam was again becoming more rigid, many people turned against Ibn'Arabi and today you could be imprisoned in Saudi Arabia for bringing his books into the country. Of course, that is always a recommendation. My own book had to be sold 'under the counter' in Saudi Arabia, so it's been read by a lot of people. Nonetheless many rigid Muslims have regarded and still do regard Ibn'Arabi as the heretic to end all heretics. To take a Christian parallel: I remember when I was in the diplomatic service in Trinidad, a very dear Catholic friend of mine, my opposite number in the American Embassy, was in my home and he happened to open a copy of Eckhart at a page where the Master was saying in effect that God's existence depends on our existence, which of course is something Ibn'Arabi also says: the personal God depends on persons, the Creator depends on a creation. Anyway, my friend flung the book across the room in a fury of outrage. Well, this is often the reaction to Ibn'Arabi today.

I'd like now to say a word about the contemporary situation in Islam. In a purely worldly sense Islam was immensely successful right up to the time Napoleon landed in Alexandria. Suddenly, everything went wrong. People who believed that they were the natural bosses of the world, and had been so for centuries, suddenly found themselves the victims of imperialism, foreign domination, foreign superiority; they were made to feel very inferior indeed. This was, of course, the most traumatic experience imaginable. Ever since then there has been a sense of trying to find someone to blame, and sometimes the Muslims blame the Sufis. They say, 'The Sufis made us too peaceful, too meditative, too thoughtful; they deprived us of our virility; if it hadn't been for these wretched Sufis we'd have conquered the rest of the world. The Sufis encouraged people to dream and to try to come close to God. You can't come close to God. God is up there and we are down here. That's that.'—and so on. This is a really ludicrous attitude if you read some Islamic history.

Let me end this section by mentioning my hero—I don't usually have heroes—Abdul-Qadir, a young Algerian, son of a Sufi *shaikh*, himself a young man of extraordinary spiritual potential and entirely a contemplative. In the mid-1820s the French invaded Algeria, the ruler collapsed, the official religious authorities acquiesced. Abdul-Qadir's father told him, 'I'm a bit too old for this, so you must gather the tribes and lead them against the French.' This young man then put down his books and unwillingly mounted his charger, gathered the tribes by some extraordinary charismatic quality he possessed, and gave the French the only really tough fight they had in their process of colonial expansion: twenty years of guerilla warfare. Those were still to some extent the days of chivalry, so, having defeated, captured and imprisoned him, the French made him a Chevalier de la Légion d'Honneur because he had been such a worthy foe. They then exiled him to Damascus, where he lived to a great age, interpreting the works of Ibn'Arabi. This scholar and mystic was called into action only once more when Druze tribesmen descended upon Damascus, determined to massacre the Christians. Abdul-Qadir then took all the Christians in the city into his own home and the Druze did not dare to attack because this man was held in such respect. So much for these poor passive Sufis who prevented Islam from fighting back!

There is also a 'popular Sufism' that manifests itself in ways which seem to me to be harmless but which shock conventional Muslims. I think particularly of a *hadrah* (meeting) I went to of the Burkaniyyah Tariquah in Cairo. For some reason this *tariquah* is composed mainly of taxi drivers: a working class *tariquah*. They come there after a very hard and exhausting day's work and they let themselves go. They have this very African technique of going 'Hah, hah, hah' for a long, long time until some of them fall down in a swoon.

Now, as I have sometimes said to my dear strict Muslims when they tell me how dreadful this is, 'Do you think it would be preferable for them to be out running after girls or drinking in the café?'

Then they have to say, 'Well, perhaps you are right, but it's very un-Islamic.'

The point is that they are doing this in honour of God and out of love for the Prophet, so I'm prepared to give three cheers for them. But I do understand why very strict Muslims are horrified by this. The fact remains that, without the Sufi dimension, Islam would be incomplete, merely a matter of legalistic observance. The legalistic form of religion, of course, has its effectiveness for certain people, but it is only half the religion; the other half is the religion of mysticism, devotion and piety which finds its full expression in Sufism.

Sufi practice is based upon two things: *faqr* and *dhikr*. I do not usually quote Buddhist principles, but there is one Buddhist principle which I quote constantly when I talk about religion and that is 'the marriage of wisdom and method': *prajña* and *upaya*. The whole practice of Sufism also consists of the balance of wisdom and method.

When I was a student my attention was drawn to a book by L.H.Myers, a well-known name at that time but forgotten now. I read a review which said Myers was the only true philosophical novelist that this country had ever produced, so I read *The Root and the Branch* and was utterly bowled over. 'At last I've found a man who is wise enough to satisfy me for the rest of my life,' I thought. And the wisdom came from his understanding of Hindu Vedanta particularly, in which I was also interested. I wrote to Myers—I was eighteen, he was sixty-two at the time—and my letter arrived at a very strange moment in his life, when he had cut himself off from old friends and was very lonely. But here was a young admirer who seemed to understand him, so he wrote back at once. Before very long we were writing each other long letters every week and I met him, in fact, three times. But even then I was finding in his letters a note of despair and desperation, which seemed very strange. At one point he wrote to me:

'I think the remark in your last letter that I put all the serenity of which I am capable into my books and left none over for myself may be rather shrewd.'

So suddenly this wonderful, wise, free man was a very disturbed man, and this was very upsetting for a young man who thought he had found security in this friendship. And then Leo Myers committed suicide, the ultimate act of despair, and in his case perhaps despair for no good reason: I think he just couldn't stand growing old. As I discovered later, he'd led a most extraordinary life of sexual adventure, but obviously a certain time comes when that is fading or disappearing. So all his wisdom had been just in the head and not backed up by any kind of practice at all; it was wisdom without method.

Now as to *faqr* and *dhikr*—*faqr* literally means poverty, in this case spiritual poverty; *dhikr* has two meanings, remembrance and invocation.

The idea of spiritual poverty is, of course, universal, but perhaps it has a very special place in Islam. To sense the presence of God within I have got to empty myself of myself—obviously not the core of my being, not of the inner nucleus which makes me what I am, but of the ego: its needs, dreams, thoughts, hopes, fears and all the rest must go. The clearing of the heart, sometimes called the polishing of the mirror (a term often used by the Prophet), this is *faqr*. It prepares the way for *dhikr*.

I think Western Christianity is the only religious path which I know of that doesn't have the equivalent of a *mantra*. Eastern Christianity has it in the Jesus Prayer, and a great many Western Christians, including some Protestants, have introduced this into their religious practice. In Islam you can use the confession of faith just as others would use a *mantra*, but basically the invocation is of the divine name, Allah. 'God' is just a word, 'Allah' is a revealed name: it is the name by which, for us, God has called himself, and He has said in both Koran and Hadith that, 'I am present when my worshipper makes mention of me.' Therefore to invoke the divine name is to make ourselves aware of that presence.

Just to sit down or to walk or to lie down and keep invoking the name of Allah would not possibly take you very far, therefore various meditations are attached to this invocation and those turn upon the 'Divine Names' the names given to God or which He gives Himself in the Koran. You may meditate upon the First and the Last: He Who is Before Time and He Who Is After Time and, needless to say, He Who Is Master of Time. You may meditate upon the All-Merciful, the Subtle, the Gently All-Penetrating (everywhere present). There are in fact slightly more than ninety-nine Names in the Koran, and these are subjects for meditation including, in the particular technique I follow, the names al-Qabid, He Who Confines, and al-Mumit, the Slayer, because meditation upon death, upon the brevity of life, is a very important thing in Islam—and not only for Sufis.

Muhammad, when asked, 'How do you polish the heart; how do you get rid of the rust, the debris from the heart?', replied, 'By remembrance of God and much thought of death.'

Also, one of the earliest Caliphs, al-Walid, had a signet ring inscribed with the letters, 'Walid, thou must die'.

This life is, in comparison with Reality, an illusion, and we must understand well that it is short and will end. Our sense of proportion is dependent upon that realization.

The Organic Paradigm and Social Order
Harry Rutherford

WHAT ESSENTIALLY IS AN ORGANISM? It is a system of relationships; a whole consisting of parts such that, while each has a distinctive character of its own and develops in accordance with that character, the parts are so related to one another that together their respective developments constitute the development of the whole, each part being itself a sub-organism. It follows from this that the parts are related to one another, not externally like the parts of a machine, but internally in such a way that any change in any part of an organism is reflected in every other part. This must, of course, be taken as a description only, not as a precise definition.

This inter-relatedness has been more than ever brought home to popular thinking by the ecological movement and by some 'advances' in medical science. It is becoming evident to people that you cannot treat the human body or any aspect of nature like a machine. The use of chemicals to change one part in a desired way will inevitably have effects on every other part, and sometimes effects that are far from desirable.

What has not yet fully struck many people is the revolution in thinking that this realization demands. The type of thinking that is based on our everyday commonsense, or dualistic, logic —what one might call billiard ball mechanical thinking—is good enough for dealing with inorganic matter by physical or chemical means, but it does not apply to organic life. Now, it can prove disastrous ecologically to try to cope with our environment with this kind of thinking. We need a radical change: far more radical than most ordinary 'greens' have envisaged. What is the nature of this change? In what way does organic thinking differ from our ordinary everyday matter-of-fact thinking?

This everyday thinking which we take for granted is simply expressed in what are known as the Laws of Thought. Briefly they consist of three simple propositions. They are: first, that anything is what it is; second that it cannot have a certain attribute and at the same time not have it; and third that it must either have a particular attribute or not have it—there is no halfway house.

As an example, a flower is a flower. However many different kinds of flower there may be, the word 'flower' always means flower. And 'red' means red—however many shades of red you can think of. Secondly this flower cannot be both red and not red at the same time. But thirdly it must either be red or not red. All our normal thinking is based on these simple propositions, which start with the notion that the same word always means the same thing. If it didn't all our everyday discourse and thinking would be impossible.

This thinking applies perfectly to a world in which there are fixed things which always stay the same. But we know that in the real world they are always changing: nothing ever stays the same in reality. Nevertheless in the world of inorganic things, they stay the same for the most part long enough to be adequately dealt with by this logic. And for the most part inorganic things are related externally to one another, like billiard balls.

These relationships may be very complex, like chemical or electrical changes, but they are still essentially susceptible to the logic of duality. A good example of this is the computer, which can do the most fantastic things but still consists in the end of millions of little bits that either say 'yes' or 'no' and affect one another only externally. You may even simulate aspects of organic working with a computer, but you cannot actually make a computer work organically.

When we come to an organism we find that the attempt to use this logic can be—and indeed has been—disastrous. So we have to think differently. We are in a world of continuous change. Everything is developing the whole time, and all changes in one part of an organism are reflected innerly in every other part of the organism. This is equally true both of the smallest organism and of the whole planet, which we have to learn to look upon as an organism.

So we have to stop thinking of fixed things which affect one another externally. We are in a world of continuous change and of processes interweaving within one another. The dualistic thinking which says that something either *is* or *is not*, that any statement is either true or false, applies to the Euclidean space in which we normally live our lives. Two things cannot be in the same place at the same time. But it does not apply to an organism. It does not even apply to motion, of which Zeno with his riddle of the arrow in flight purported to have proved the impossibility. According to the Laws of Thought motion is indeed impossible, because at every moment in its flight the arrow is where it is, so how does it get to where it is not?

An organism is born, develops through a lifetime, and finally dies. The ancient Indians represented these three phases of life by three gods: Brahma, Vishnu and Shiva. Organic thinking has to be trinitarian, not dualistic. Instead of saying that something *either* is *or* is not, we have to conceive the possibility that it *both* is *and* is not. The fact that every statement can be contradicted implies that it is too narrow a view to say that anything must be either true or false. It may be both true and false. From the moment an organism is born the forces of life and those of death are both working within it. The result is the development of the organism. Every organism develops in a state of continuous tension between opposing forces.

Providence—or whatever you choose to call the inner power in the Universe—has given us the morphology of organism as the pattern of all life. We did not invent it. It would be possible to suggest that it developed altogether by accident, and indeed if anyone were to assert that it did, it would be impossible to disprove it. But if that were true, life itself would be meaningless. It would be a series of accidents rather than an ordered development, and so could have no possible goal, unless humanity could get together and invent one, which would in such circumstances be too improbable.

Providence—again we use the word only as the most neutral we can find; it need not be thought of as a Being—also developed life up to the physical, psychic, spiritual organism of the human being. Undoubtedly we did not invent ourselves. But we have now reached the stage where we can no longer rely on Providence to show us how we should develop further. We have attained the possibility of exercising free will and have reached a stage in human development where a true social order can exist only by the free will of its constituent individuals. It is now our responsibility to perform the next creative act and create a new social order.

The best that we have so far achieved is democracy, but that is clearly inadequate. As Professor Parkinson once pointed out, the time when democracy flourished best in the world was between the wars; since then all our attempts at democracy end up, as Plato showed in the *Republic*, in dictatorship, whether imposed by force or, as Lord Hailsham described our British democracy, 'elective'. The trouble about democracy is that it is not a real life form. Any application of it is purely quantitative and mechanical, depending as it does on the counting of votes. It cannot satisfy the desire which most people have to participate actively in making the decisions which directly affect them.

But though it is up to us to create social order, we do not have to invent the form of it. That is already given to us in the morphology of organism. We only have to work out how to apply it in practice. The most fundamental problem of our social life is the relationship between the individual and the community. Which should take precedence? The answer is neither one nor the other but both, sinced they are inter-dependent. The community is an abstraction apart from its constituent individuals, and no individual can be fully developed who is not properly integrated into the community. In an organism every organ and every single cell perform their proper function within the whole by behaving according to its own inner nature. There is no conflict between the good of the whole and that of the parts.

This principle is best embodied socially in the twin principles of devolution and federation. Devolution means that every decision is made in the smallest group of those who are directly concerned with the effects of its implementation; federation means that any such decision is taken only after adequate consultation with all other groups of individuals who may be affected. This is the exact opposite of our present hierarchical system, as operated in democracies, that every decision is taken at as high a level as is necessary to take into account the interests of all concerned.

In almost all institutions within our present democratic system the necessary guide is the organization chart. This dictates strict lines of command from the top to the bottom, modified only by some functional lines of responsibility. This approach to what is wrongly called organization is the opposite of organic. An organism is wholly functional with no part of it having direct control over any other.

In every physical organism from the smallest cell to the most developed (e.g. the human body), there are three major functions. It takes in nourishment and excretes unwanted matter; it receives sense impressions, to which it reacts; and it breathes. This triunity of major functions is more obvious in the more developed organisms and clearest of all in the human organism. Translated into terms of our social life, these three major functions correspond to economics, culture and politics respectively.

The metabolic system, which takes in food and converts it into energy, represents the economics of our body. The nervous system, centred in the brain, which is the material foundation for our consciousness, corresponds to culture. These two are normally in conflict with one another: the metabolic system produces, our consciousness consumes. The relating function in our social life between our economic needs and our cultural aspirations, and between the demands and requirements of all the different groups in society, is politics. This is represented by our respiratory, circulatory system, which distributes the energy produced by our metabolic system throughout the whole body, giving to each part according to its needs. As blood circulates in the human body to distribute the wealth which has been produced, so money should circulate freely in the social order to distribute wealth where it is needed. It does not do this at present because those who create money, namely the banks and financial institutions, demand a premium for creating something out of nothing.

As in the human body the three major functions, though centred in different parts of the body, namely the stomach, head and heart respectively, nevertheless permeate the body, interweaving with one another in every single part of it; so in our social life there should be three main separate centres to direct our economic, cultural and political lives. But they should be looked upon, not as three ruling bodies, but as the centres of three different systems or kinds of process, each working according to its own principles, and all three pervading the whole social system and related to one another in every region, village or individual person.

This can at best be only a sketch. It is necessary above all to remember that it has to be considered organically and not mechanically. It must therefore grow organically, and cannot be superimposed on our present hierarchical ideas of government or management. The essence of it is in devolution and federation, with the greatest possible freedom for every section of it, every grouping of persons for every economic, cultural or social purpose, and for every individual. All decisions will be made in the smallest possible group of those affected and at the same time there will be continuous consultation and discussion between all the different groups concerned.

It is quite clear that this would not be a starter with our present confrontational modes of behaviour and thinking, just as the dreams of the ecologists are wholly impracticable without radical changes in our whole life style, in the pattern of our desires and our thinking. So what are the main changes in our consciousness which would be required to make such a social order possible?

This can be summarized under two main headings, which relate to our thinking on the one hand and to our willing and feeling on the other. We cannot change our feelings directly. They are as they are. We can, however, control them indirectly through our thinking and our actions.

The change needed in our thinking is to do so organically rather than by formal, mechanistic logic. We have to think in terms of processes rather than fixed points; we have to have ideas which are flexible, not rigid; something is not necessarily right or wrong, true or false. Change has to be admitted into one's thinking as well as continuity and consistency. Perhaps the most succinct way of expressing this is to look at the question of truth.

The common notion of truth is that it is objective; that it is what is the case independently of what any human being may think. The opposite view, held by many, is that it is subjective: that it depends only on what we individuals think. The radical change towards organic thinking is to realize that truth is neither objective—it is in itself a purely human notion and does not exist apart from what individuals think. Nor is it merely subjective—it does not depend on what any individual thinks. It is intra-subjective; that is to say, it depends on agreement between individuals. Truth is therefore not a fixed thing, nor is it purely arbitrary. It is social and develops as all our different human points of view converge towards agreement by a process of approximation.

The other main change is referred to in Book v of the *Republic*, where Plato affirms that what binds a city together is community of pleasure and pain, when all citizens rejoice and grieve over the common gains and losses; where 'our' supersedes 'mine'. Or as Erich Gutkind puts it, describing what he means by the much abused and misused word 'socialism': 'The *I* must perish but *we* must put forth life.' But this, he affirms, is not any loss of individuality; on the contrary, it can be achieved only by the most fully developed personality. It is what throughout the New Testament is called love. Without love there could be no organic functioning. As Dimitrije Mitrinović expressed it, 'All things and beings are for the sake of one another and through one another. Divinity is the glory and perfection of their unity and co-functioning.'

Vladimir Solovyov in his book *The Meaning of Love* wrote that, 'The falsity and evil of egoism does not consist in the fact that a person creates himself with unconditional significance and infinite worth, but in the fact that, rating himself rightly as unconditionally significant, he unjustly refuses this same significance to others . . . The meaning of love as a feeling consists in this, that it constrains us to acknowledge for another the unconditional central significance of which, in virtue of our egoism, we are conscious only in ourselves.'

In the earliest days of human development a tribal family consciousness was more present to individuals than their own individual consciousness. This was purely instinctive—one might say individually almost unconscious. Through many millennia we have developed individual self-consciousness and this has now reached an extreme of disruptive individualism in parts of the Western world. The next necessary stage in human development, the true meaning of socialism, is that while fully retaining our individual awareness and freedom, our awareness of being part of a community should become as strong as our feeling of individuality. It will then no longer be a question of one aspect taking precedence over or subordinating the other. Then, as in organism, each individual will find the true fulfilment of his or her own nature to be identical with the fulfilment of function within the whole community.

Such shared consciousness is indeed far away from anything we can imagine now, but it is a necessary development if the human goal of a community of free individuals is to be attained. Remote though it may be, it can even now provide us with a regulative ideal, like a beacon shining from afar.

In Search of the Guru
Shenpen Hookham

TIME AND AGAIN I FIND MYSELF engaged in explaining certain general principles of the practice of Triyana Buddhism that Tibetan lamas take so much for granted they seldom, if ever, explain. Nevertheless, when they discover their students do not understand these principles they are literally horrified and wonder how Westerners are ever going to relate to the teachings properly. Seeing this makes me feel very sad and, when I think about it, I realize that if someone like myself, who sees the problem, does not do anything about it, then who will?

Let us start with a hypothetical person on the street who hears, perhaps, a radio programme on Buddhism which inspires him/her to seek out a Buddhist teacher. What does he/she do?

He/she assumes that, since Buddhism is a long established religion, there is an established hierarchy of authority reflected in the status and titles given to teachers. This is a mistaken assumption. There is not one established hierarchy of authority and no standardization of status and titles across all Buddhist traditions. There is no head of any of the main schools of Buddhism, such as Theravada, Mahayana, Vajrayana, Zen and so on. Even within a single tradition within these major schools there are more often than not inconsistencies in the way titles such as lama, tulku, ngagpa, rimpoche, bhikkhu, venerable, reverend, roshi, etc., are used and adopted. The truth of the matter is that one cannot rely on titles to discover who are the authentic and experienced spiritual representatives of a tradition. Often, particularly these days, people have adopted titles to give themselves an air of authority. This may have been necessary in order to be effective in their particular situation, whereas someone else, equally if not more worthy of a title, may use none at all.

Since one cannot refer to any central authority, nor rely on titles, one would be forgiven for assuming that in Buddhism there is no authority and that either nobody is more qualified and experienced than anyone else or nobody knows who the authentic teachers are. This is also a mistake. In fact in a number of Buddhist traditions it is possible, by asking the right questions of the right people, to discover quite precisely who are the most experienced and advanced teachers on any particular area or level. This is certainly the case in 'Tibetan' Buddhism. I have used inverted commas because it is misleading to talk of Tibetan Buddhism as if it were something other than Indian Triyana Buddhism and as if all traditions of Triyana Buddhism in Tibet are the same. There are some very important differences between them.

So who are the right people to ask and what are the questions one should be asking? In the Tibetan traditions, the people to ask are the main holders of the lineage. Each lineage has a number of senior teachers who are respected by everyone within the lineage. First one has to find out who these people are. Then one has to find out which lamas these teachers go to for teaching and advice. Then you have discovered the 'top-league' as it were. This group of lamas will know from their own judgement which of the 'up-and-coming' practitioners have reached a high level of realization and are good Dharma practitioners. These 'up-and'coming' practitioners may be very advanced and be with or without title and status, or they may be a little advanced with or without title and status. If you want to discover the relative status of these people as practitioners, you have to ask such questions as, 'Is that person *tsa chenpo*?' In other words, 'Is he a powerful source of spiritual strength and connection?' If the answer is in the affirmative, you then have to ask, 'Is he

as *tsa chenpo* as the head of the lineage or one of the teachers
of the head of the lineage?' The answer to this may be a little
laugh and an explanation of just how *tsa chenpo* the head of
the lineage is and how only 'top-league' lamas can compare
with them. So then you lower your threshold to some lama
whom you know is universally recognized as a 'good lama'.
Ask if the lama in question is as *tsa chenpo* as that. You will
gradually learn by the response to your questions which lamas
are more or less in the same running and which lamas are simply
out of the running as far as *tsa chenpo* is concerned. A lama or
teacher or practitioner who is not *tsa chenpo* in any special sense
is an ordinary person whose quality of connection with Dharma
you can judge for yourself by working with them and getting to
know them. A lama, teacher or practitioner who is *tsa chenpo*
may or may not turn out to have extraordinary qualities as far
as you are concerned. You are advised, on the one hand, to treat
any encounter with such a person as a blessing while, on the other
hand, if too much association with the person causes your faith
to wither and fall away, quietly keep a distance. You maintain
your own integrity and judgement by seeing clearly whether the
relationship with this person works for you or not. You avoid
hasty judgements arising out of your own lack of connection and
experience by keeping a distance if things start to go wrong.

In the above section I have tried to give a rough guide for
someone encountering one of the Tibetan traditions. Perhaps
other principles are needed when approaching other traditions.
The general principle for everyone is, however, that one seeks a
good teacher much as one seeks out anything of great value. One
has to find out a lot about the context or milieu in which it is to
be found and to look and check carefully before assuming you
have found the right thing. Much can be learnt as one looks and
checks and this is all part of the processs of spiritual awakening.
It is not time wasted or something to be regretted or hurried over.
At all times it is important to seek in as genuine a way as you

can, noticing your own pride, prejudice and ignorance as you do so. Do not, however, think that your own judgement in the matter has to be abandoned for some higher authority. If you find yourself unable to trust your own judgement, you will, by the same count, be unable to practise Dharma.

There is an important point that one has to bear in mind when questioning members of the lineage on the merits of different practitioners, because to neglect to do so could easily lead to endless confusion. It is common practice and, in fact, a beautiful and powerful practice, for Tibetans and I am sure others to speak of someone displaying in part the qualities of the bodhisattvas as being indeed a bodhisattva. It is rather like we might say, 'He's a real angel', or 'He's my guardian angel.' Maybe we say such things rather lightly but it is possible that someone who believed in guardian angels might actually feel that a person who has helped him was in fact an expression of the general protective activity of his guardian angel. In the same way a Tibetan or a Tibetan lama might say of someone being kind in some way such as by taking a dog to the vet, 'He is a real bodhisattva'. Someone who helps a lot of people, maybe simply by using their influence and saying the right thing at the right moment, might be called, 'An emanation of Tara.' This is not sarcasm; it is heartfelt. Similarly they may say of someone earnestly practising Dharma that they are *tsa chenpo*. What they mean is that the most powerful way to help beings is to practise the Dharma and since this person has chosen to do this he is a vehicle for the power and blessing of the Dharma. The principle can be extended endlessly. I have personally experienced being called 'rimpoche' when embarking on a long retreat, or 'bodhisattva' when trying to help others understand Dharma, 'ngagpa' on account of having given up my nun's robes and even 'omniscient Dolpopa' by Kalu Rimpoche in the context of my doctoral thesis in which I champion the doctrine taught by Dolpopa. In the last case there was of course an element of mischievous humour there, especially when my husband got addressed as Dolpopa's wife. Nevertheless, there is also a sense in which the activity of the omniscient Dolpopa lives through the work I have done on Shentong, and I know from experience that Tibetans genuinely think in this way. It is so natural to them that they do not think of explaining what they mean. If you were to say, 'I'm not really *tsa chenpo*, am I?' they might insist that you are and quote proverbs and stories showing how, by their thinking that you are, they acquire spiritual merit even if it turns out that you are not a genuine practitioner. A favourite story often quoted in this context is that of the *tsa tsa*. This is a story of how an old lady treated a dog's tooth as *tsa chenpo* because she thought it was a tooth of the Buddha. Because of her faith, the power and blessing of the Buddha was able to reach her though the vehicle of the tooth and she became enlightened. The point of such stories is that even if, in spite of your efforts to find a genuine teacher, you end up putting all your trust in someone unworthy, the blessing of the Buddha can still reach you via that person if your faith and devotion to that person are genuine enough. That is why it is always best to treat any problems you may have with a spiritual teacher with great care. This is especially the case if you actually receive some sort of teaching or inspiration from them. You may subsequently find that person has faults you cannot abide. The only thing to do in that case is to retire to a safe distance and remember only the positive aspects of the relationship.

The biggest problem then is to decide how much responsibility one has to warn others of the dangers you have yourself encoun-tered by getting too involved with that particular teacher. On this point I can offer no advice. Tibetans, generally speaking, opt for saying as little as possible for fear of stirring up negative emotions —their own and others. Since it is easy enough for a Tibetan to find out about teachers by associating with the right people and asking a few discreet questions, there is no need for Tibetans to say much to each other concerning such matters. It is more difficult for Westerners because they do not speak Tibetan and do not know the conventions.

For example, the convention for putting down a teacher who, although scarcely qualified, has many disciples is to only ever speak of his many disciples and never of his qualities. So when you ask, 'Is he *tsa chenpo*?', the answer might be, 'He has many disciples.' If he were really *tsa chenpo* the answer would have been something like, 'Oh yes, he trained at such a monastery and has such and such teachers, and has much meditational realization and experience.' On the other hand, if you say, 'My teacher is Lama T. He's a wonderful lama isn't he?', you can be sure no Tibetan is going to tell you otherwise. It is fundamental to their whole way of thinking that they should never undermine a person's faith. After all, the story of the *tsa tsa* shows that faith is the most important thing. A good lama in whom you have no faith can do less for you then a bad one through whom you get some genuine spiritual experience.

This is all unfamiliar territory for Westerners and somehow it seems bizarre that a tradition can boast great teachers and siddhas and great technical knowledge of the stages of the path to enlightenment and yet tolerate and even praise quite dubious characters in order not to disturb the faith of their followers. To us, this insistence on the quality of faith being more important than the quality of the teacher indicates a lack of the need for proper spiritual direction. After all, if one's own faith is sufficient, what need is there for expert advice and guidance? This is also a mistake. A Tibetan would be horrified to think that such a message was being conveyed to Westerners through what he had said. Yet one sees it happening again and again. So what message is a Tibetan trying to convey through his attitude to dubious teachers? It is that the power of Dharma is so great that sometimes (which is in fact rarely) it can happen that in spite of a bad teacher a particularly gifted disciple can reach enlightenment. The chances against such an event are enormous but the story serves to illustrate a principle. The principle is that if you are having difficulty with a spiritual relationship, you had better face the fact that you are not an especially gifted person and so had better make sure you find a really genuine and experienced teacher with whom you can have a relationship that works. The most important thing is that the relationship works and that you find your mind opening and shifting from gross to ever subtler understandings of the Dharma and its significance in your life and the lives of others.

It often happens that a person seeking to become involved in a Buddhist tradition finds himself in the presence of a teacher who gives him some definite advice. It is not always clear on what basis this advice is being given. For example in some Tibetan centres the Western disciples of a Tibetan lama will often tell you that you must do as the lama says with dire warnings of what happens to those who do not. The implication is that there is some divine plan to which the lama is privy, and he has the extraordinary power to know for each person what part he has to play in this plan. If the lama tells you to live in a certain place, marry a certain person, do a certain retreat, do a certain job and so on, then that is what it is ordained that you should do.

Why should we believe this? Buddhism has no doctrine of pre-destination, divine plan or fate. Yet sometimes one detects a hint of such doctrines in the way people understand karma. Actually karma means action. Action implies not only a deed but also its effect. Wealth and good fortune are called good karma after their cause, generous actions. Poverty and bad luck are called bad karma after their cause, mean actions. When the lama gives advice he may simply be advising us in the direction of good actions. In that case it would not matter what one did as long as it was a good action. Generally speaking, however, when a lama gives advice he is thinking of the whole situation that he is working in. He is thinking if what would be good for the whole community of his disciples. He more often than not has some long term goal in mind, a certain direction he wants to work towards. You are not obliged to follow his direction unless you particularly want to become involved in that particular lama's activity, his circle as it were. On the other hand, if you do wish to get involved you have to accept that the essential point is that you are serving the lama and seeking to realize his vision. It may seem to you that what he wants to do is bizarre and the way he approaches it self-defeating. You might well be right too. The history of Buddhism is not one of infallibility—not even the Buddha was able to solve everything for everyone. In fact, when one reads the details of the life of the Buddha and the way the community evolved, it is clear that the Buddha dealt with people in a very human way and things did go wrong, fairly frequently it would seem.

The point is that once you decide to get involved with a teacher you are involving yourself in a relationship. You carry out his wishes, discuss with him the options, feed back to him the effects of what he is doing and what he has said, make apologies when you are not able to fulfil his wishes, explaining why and so on. In other words, one relates to him with respect and sensitivity as one would in any relationship. This will stimulate a response from the teacher. The relationship will deepen and a sense of trust will develop. Even an enlightened teacher has to be drawn out and stimulated to teach, so how much more so a teacher who is still in training himself. The disciples have a vital part to play in bringing down the enlightened activity of the Buddhas into the world and enabling it to be effective. For this reason one should not approach a teacher with preconceived ideas about how an enlightened teacher would think or behave. One approaches him with humility and a willingness to engage in a living relationship. You may as well accept that you do not know how enlightened or otherwise your chosen teacher is. This will emerge as you work with him. By allowing you to work with him the teacher is being supremely generous to you and so however it turns out you should always approach him with respect and gratitude. This is never wasted.

It does happen that sometimes a person is advised to go to a lama to get advice on a specific problem, such as a sickness or a family problem. It is more than likely that the lama will respond with some definite advice. He might do this even if he does not really have much idea of what is going on. It is a more or less unconscious cultural response to the state of indecision in a person. Since the person cannot decide what to do, you suggest something definite. That helps him to decide definitely for or against your suggestion and so helps to clear his mind. Watch out for this and do not assume the lama always knows.

Having said all this I have to admit that now and again one does meet a lama with seeming extraordinary powers for intuiting what would be the best thing for you to do in any given situation. Often this expresses itself in their doing what is called a *mo*. *Mo* is sometimes translated as 'divination'. The idea is something like casting the *I Ching*. One opens one's mind to the blessing of the Buddha's activity coming through the lineage and more or less throws a dice a number of times to receive a coded 'reply'. The problem usually has to be phrased in terms of alternatives—is this option better than that option? The 'reply' comes back as a series of graded options. To do this is best, this is very bad, none of the options is good or this option is slightly better than that and so on. Generally speaking, lamas are not keen to do *mo*s except in situations where all else fails. This reluctance stems partly from the fact that they are not always easy to interpret and so are unreliable. Also it is inappropriate and impractical to try to run everyone's lives by endless *mo*s. Nevertheless, most lamas do them on occasion and often give startlingly precise advice by means of them. Does one really have to go along with the reply of a *mo*? The point is that if you do not intend to go along with it, why are you asking for one? You obviously have a strong idea of your own of what you should do and therefore you should not have asked for a *mo* in the first place. Even if you go along with the *mo* you cannot know in what sense the indicated option is best. It may turn out in such a way that it does not seem the right thing at all. Surprisingly often, however, one finds the *mo* works pretty well. Hence its popularity. Occasionally you meet a lama who will not do a *mo* but will give you very clear, precise advice on what you should do. The advice does seem to be coming from an extraordinary intuitive power and maybe it is, but the decision is still up to you whether you want to go along with it or not.

Sometimes people get confused by stories of great tantric practitioners like Naropa, Marpa, Milarepa and so on. In these stories great emphasis is put on obedience to the lama. Perhaps this is where the idea that you should always do what the lama says comes from. The important thing to understand here is that in the case of Naropa and so on we are talking about practitioners in whom the relationship with the guru has matured. When in the story it seems that the relationship is mature from the moment the disciple meets the guru, it is implied, if not always said, that this is because of the ripening of a past karmic connection. In other words, complete obedience to the guru is necessary once the relationship has matured to a certain point and when advanced tantric techniques are being employed. Obedience out of respect is required in Hinayana and Mahayana. In other words one complies with the wishes of the guru in order to learn from him. If you stop obeying him, you stop learning from him and that is all there is to it. In Vajrayana the bond with the guru is much stronger and more vital than that. One is actually going to allow oneself to become possessed by the guru's enlightenment. Once this has started to happen there is nothing one can do to stop the process and to try to do so is to create the worst kind of hell for oneself. One obeys the guru in such a situation because not to do so is like suicide. To do so is to participate in enlightenment here and now. Tremendous confidence and maturity is required in such a relationship and one obeys the guru because of the relationship and that is all there is to it. It does not matter whether you approve or disapprove of what you are being told to do. The important thing is that you have confidence at all times that it is the enlightened activity of the Buddhas working in and through you through the power of the guru's blessing. To understand the subtleties of such tantric relationship one has to have experienced and understood the meaning of the Hinayana and Mahayana paths. Tantra is not a new path different from the foregoing ones. It is a vaster and more precise vision of what is really meant in the other two vehicles. So you have been warned.

It should be clear by now that one should at all times use one's own judgement and decision. If you have decided to enter into a certain kind of relationship, then be true to that and be consistent in your behaviour. Do not confuse yourself and others by pretending to have a deeper or more superficial relationship than is the case. Do not try to act as if you were a great yogi like Milarepa when your mind is still subject to doubts about your teacher. Do not think that just because a teacher is not enlightened that you do not owe him respect and gratitude.

Another problem I am often confronted with is people who have a lot of faith in a number of teachers and are agonizing over which of them is their 'root guru'. This is a problem specific to Tantric Buddhism, but since Tibetans always teach the practice of Buddhism from a tantric perspective the question of the root guru tends to come up very early. In fact, I have heard eminent lamas begin a public talk by telling everyone to pray to their root lama on the crown of their head as a preliminary to their listening to the talk. So what is a root lama or guru? The idea is that the guru who introduces you to the true nature of the mind actually introduces you to your own enlightenment, and since your own enlightenment is one and the same as that of the guru and of the Buddha then all the blessing that ensues from that introduction comes directly from the guru as a living presence in your life and stream of being. He epitomizes your whole connection with the Dharma and with reality itself. This is a very subtle point and very hard to understand. There are many stories of even quite advanced practitioners who did not understand it entirely. One might wonder why therefore a lama would begin his talk with such a statement. The truth of the matter seems to be that Tibetans have a simple kind of faith that enables them to link into this kind of statement at an intuitive level without too much intellectualization. So maybe it is fine for them. For us it is often very confusing.

Here are some tips for people who find themselves working within the context of Tibetan Buddhism. Do not think that anyone is your root lama until you are quite sure what it means and what such a relationship means. Be hesitant even if you are told what it means. It takes a long time to really understand and both teacher and pupil have to enter the relationship very fully and deliberately. In the meantime it is best to think of the term 'root guru' as another term for Buddha. Any teacher you meet is like an expression of the activity of the Buddha—the primordial root guru. The Buddha's activity is in one sense acting everywhere equally all the time but where it impinges on one's own life is where it counts most for you. Whenever we encounter the presence of the Buddha's teaching in the world, we can think of that as the activity of the Buddha or the root guru. Sometimes it comes through this person, sometimes another, but the source is always the Buddha, the primordial guru. One should treat all sources of Dharmic inspiration as the guru. This helps to focus one's mind towards the source of one's inspiration and develop a sense of trust and devotion. You do not have to choose one or other of a number of teachers who have helped you and go overboard in trying to feel more strongly for one guru than for another. It just is not necessary. In fact, that sort of thing is never necessary. It is never necessary to compartmentalize one's mind and try to make it feel and believe this way or that. One feels a natural devotion and it is more often than not quite diffuse, especially at first. Because it is diffuse it is difficult to concentrate one's mind and open out with prayer and devotion. So one thinks of it all concentrated into one generalized figure such as the head of the lineage, or Vajradhara, or into particular lamas with whom you have a strong connection. Thinking like this does not mean that you now have a root guru relationship in the full tantric sense of the term and there is no reason to think you have to ask that particular person what to do at every turn. All that comes in much much later if ever and even then in a completely different context.

Tibetans understand this very well and are apt not to explain the basic principles involved here. Instead they might tell you stories about exceptional events and situations where by obeying the guru exactly on some seemingly minor point leads a certain disciple to instant enlightenment. These are popular stories because they are out of the ordinary and tell us what could happen if we got it all perfectly right. Most of us do not get things right straight away and so have to work steadily and intelligently towards that goal.

If you are in the situation in which many Westerners find themselves of having received many tantric teachings and empowerments from many different teachers and felt strong waves of devotion first here and then there, having perhaps felt one was committed to this or that lama or lineage, only to find some years later one is still drifting aimlessly from lama to lama, then it is important to start taking stock of the situation. It is important to take some sort of decision. Go to one of the teachers you trust and tell him/her you want to work with him/her as your teacher. Mention to him/her the other teachers you feel particularly connected to, but make it clear that from now on you are relying on him/her for instruction. Do what he/she tells you and make apologies when you cannot. At all times make it clear that you want him/her to take responsibility for your practice.

Then think of him/her as representing all the lamas by whom you feel or have felt inspired. Think that in obeying him/her you are keeping your bond with all of them. Do not agonize over whether really you feel more devotion to this or that person. It is bound to fluctuate and you should not be surprised about that. When the time comes for you to move on, it is important to discuss it with the teacher you have been working with. Explain to him/her that you do not feel the new teacher you are going to is different from himself/herself in essence and generally keep things as tidy and focused as possible.

Lamas, Tsars and Commissars:
Buddhism in Russia
John Snelling

JUST OFF BUSY PRIMORSKY PROSPEKT in the northern Star-
aya Derevnya suburb of St Petersburg, a squat, solid building
of reddish granite stands among monotonous residential blocks
and a few high-rises put up since World War II. Rather than
the baroque and rococo that flaunt themselves in the centre of
the city, the architectural influences here are distinctly Tibeto-
Mongolian—with a dash of Art Nouveau. Though now in disre-
pair, this is a Buddhist temple, the first built in Western Europe.

But how, one might well ask, could such an anomaly come to
exist in so alien a milieu?

The answer is not difficult to uncover. As the juggernaut of the
Russian Empire expanded remorselessly during past centuries,
it casually engulfed Asiatic peoples like the Buryat, a nomadic
Mongol people who tended their herds on the steppe to the
east of Lake Baikal in eastern Siberia. A little later, in the
early eighteenth century, the Gelugpa or Yellow Hat form of
Tibetan Buddhism was transmitted to them by Tibetan and
Mongolian lamas, and subsequently Buryat lamas like Lubsan
Zhimba Akhaldayev and Damba Darzha Zayayev travelled
to Urga and Lhasa, the Mongolian and Tibetan capitals, in
order to obtain religious instruction. When they returned, a
beginning was made in ordaining indigenous lamas and building
temples (locally known as *datsan* after the Tibetan *dratsang*,
monastic college), which became numerous and important as

centres of culture, healing and education. Contrary to what might be expected, the Imperial Russian authorities were not hostile to such developments, though they were concerned to bring them under some measure of state control; so in 1741 Empress Elizabeth created the office of Khambo Lama (later Khambo Bandido Lama), the supreme head of the Buddhists of Russia, whose official seat was at Gusinoye Ozero Datsan near Selenginsk.

Another group of nomadic Mongolian Buddhists, the Kalmyks, had migrated *en masse* from Dzungaria in Central Asia to the lawless Cossack zone between the Volga and Don rivers in the early seventeenth century, and though some returned to their old homelands in 1770/1, many remained on the steppe between the cities of Stavropol and Astrakhan. In the early days of their migration they were able to maintain connections with Lhasa, the focal centre of Tibetan Buddhism, and pious Kalmyks would make the arduous journey there to pursue higher religious studies. Notable among them was Zaya Pandita, who on his return to the Kalmyk steppe translated many Tibetan texts into his native language. Connections were broken from early eighteenth to the late nineteenth centuries, however, and though there was then something of a temporary revival, the Kalmyks were for practical purposes too far out on a limb ever to be properly integrated with the Tibetan Buddhist mainstream.

Finally, Buddhism entered into a unique syncretism with the traditional ecstatic shamanism of the Mongols in Tannu-Tuva, a remote region that once fell within the confines of Outer Mongolia but which was finally annexed to the USSR in 1944. According to Russian observers, in one region of Tannu-Tuva the chief lama was married to the great shamaness.

The presence of ethnic Buddhists within the confines of the Russian empire led to significant developments in European Russia. Notably, scholarship was stimulated, so that academics like I.P. Minayev. S.F. Oldenburg, O. Rosenberg and F.I. Stcher-batsky (whose classic *Buddhist Logic*, written in English, is still in print today) became pioneers in Buddhist studies, especially in the translation and study of Mahayana texts. The Oriental Institute of the Russian (later the USSR) Academy of Sciences supported their efforts and a Biblioteca Buddhica was set up to publish their works. From 1928 to 1930 there was even an Institute of Buddhist Culture, of which Stcherbatsky was director. At the same time, many European Russian sophis-ticates and intellectuals, feeling the limitations of Orthodox Christianity, were casting around for new spiritual directions, and some were attracted to Buddhist philosophy, with the result that in St Petersburg, the old capital, a Buddhist com-munity composed of Buryat and Kalmyk Buddhists and Rus-sian sympathizers emerged around the turn of the century. There were political repercussions too, for those in high pol-icy circles who advocated Russian expansion in Asia—notable among them was the influential newspaper owner and editor Prince E.E. Ukhtomsky—were not slow to see the potential for exploiting Buryat and Kalmyk connections with Mongolia and Tibet.

The outstanding modern Russian Buddhist is Agvan Dorzhiev (1854-1938), who studied at Drepung monastic university near Lhasa and achieved such a reputation for philosophical virtuosity that he was appointed a *tzenshab* or assistant tutor to the Thir-teenth Dalai Lama. He also exerted political influence, urging the young prelate to look to Russia for support against the encroachments of British and Manchu China. Dorzhiev's various quasi-diplomatic missions to Russia, when he spoke personally with the last Tsar, Nicholas II, reignited old British fears of Russian designs on India and was one of the causes of Colonel Younghusband's invasion of Tibet in 1904.

Dorzhiev used his legendary diplomatic skills to obtain per-mission to build the Buddhist temple mentioned above. The considerable costs were to be met by contributions from the Dalai Lama, the Buryats and Kalmyks, and from Inner and Outer Mongolia. The project gestated for a number of years before actual construction began around 1909. There was, understandably, considerable resistance to the idea of building a heathen temple in Christian Petersburg, particularly from ultra right-wing groups like the Union of the Russian People. Dorzhiev, a man of considerable will power, was not to be deflected, however, and the temple was finally completed and inaugurated in 1915. It is a splendid building with two main constituent parts: a two-storey *dukhang* incorporating the main monastic assembly hall, and a real section of four storeys with the *gonkhang* or protector chapel situated at the top, above the level of the *dukhang* roof. By all accounts in its heyday it was replete with treasures, including a gilded statue of the Buddha donated by King Rama vi of Siam. As it was moreover intended to be a working *datsan* rather than a mere showcase, it was staffed by lamas, who were lodged in an adjacent building.

Two years after the consecration of the temple, the Bolshevik Revolution shook the world and turned Russia on its head. Contrary to what might be thought, however, the early years of the soviet régime were a period of liberation for Russian Buddhists, particularly in Buryatia, where valiant attempts were made to work out an accommodation between Buddhism and Bolshevism. Buddhism, it was argued, was 'scientific'; it worshipped no creator God and so was 'a religion of atheism'; it was a valid cultural expression of some minority peoples; and, just like Marxism, it was compassionately concerned that 'the weak should not be oppressed but cared for'. Some Buddhists even went so far as to claim that the Buddha, not Lenin, was the founder of communism! In Agvan Dorzhiev, Russian Buddhists moreover had an able champion who could bandy Marxist-Leninist scripture to effect with party functionaries at both the central and local levels. There is evidence that the great lama was initially inspired by the idealistic atmosphere generated by the two revolutions of 1917, and particularly welcomed the granting of religious freedom and equality—formerly the Orthodox Church had been privileged—and the notion that national minorities be given the right to self-determination. During the early 1920s striving to work with a new régime that had clearly come to stay, he moved well over to the left of his own church to become the leader of a radical reform movement that advocated that lamas renounce their fine robes, possessions and privileges, and return to the austerity of a kind of idealized early Buddhism. The overall result was a Buddhist revival, and in eastern Siberia during the period new temples were opened, old ones renovated and numbers of lamas soared to thousands.

Unfortunately all this was short-lived, for in 1929 Stalin launched his reign of terror against ideological and class opponents throughout the USSR. Anti-Buddhist diatribes began almost at once to appear in the party press, and the Buryat branch of the Militant Godless declared that 'Buddhist atheism has nothing to do with militant atheism based on the Marxist appraisal of the laws of nature and society.' At first monasteries were subjected to heavy taxation; then, 'in response to a popular vote of the Buryat workers,' they began to be closed; later they were all destroyed—121 of them in Buryatia in a single year, and not by imported heavies but by local youth, who regarded the destruction as great fun. Lamas, meanwhile, were initially forced to return to lay life; then they were arrested and sent to prison camps; finally, liquidations began. As for the St Petersburg temple, the last ceremony was held there in 1933 and in 1938 it was commandeered by the state.

Despite his diplomatic and survival skills, Agvan Dorzhiev also fell from grace with the authorities, who, in 1931, fearing that he might foment trouble among his fellow Buryat, forced him to leave his native Trans-Baikalia. He then lived in a *dacha* at Olgino, just beyond the northern peripheries of St Petersburg but not far from his temple. One night in 1937 Black Marias drew up at the house beside the temple, officers entered the building and took the remaining lamas away to NKVD headquarters on Liteinyi Prospekt. They were summarily tried by three man NKVD tribunals on charges arising under the notorious Article 58 of the Criminal Code, found guilty and sentenced to death. None of the conventional niceties of justice would have been observed. According to the standard practice, they would have been taken down to the sound-proofed cellars of the building the same night and shot in the back of the head at point-blank range. Afterwards, their bodies were driven away for burial in mass graves on waste land at Levashovo on the northern edge of the city. Many Russian Orientalists suffered a similar fate.

Soon afterwards, having returned to Buryatia, Dorzhiev was also arrested on various charges under Article 58, including leading a Pan-Mongolian terrorist organization. Mercifully the Buddhist equivalent of divine intercession occurred: before anything worse could happen, he fell ill and on January 29th 1938 died of cardiac arrest in the prison hospital at Ulan-Ude, the Buryat capital. His body was duly returned to his relatives, who buried him, according to Buryat custom, in the forest.

During the so-called Great Patriotic War (1941-45), a particularly poignant tragedy befell the Kalmyks. Because a few collaborated with the invading Germans, the full brunt of Stalin's draconian fury descended upon the whole nation, and in 1948 as many as ten thousand were deported to the arctic wastes of Siberia, where countless died. Those who were lucky managed to escape abroad, and exile communities were set up, principally in Germany and in the United States. Those who remained in the USSR were not allowed to return to the Lower Volga Region until after Stalin's death.

The Buryat fared rather better. In order to secure their support for the war effort, Stalin was obliged to grant concessions; so, for pragmatic reasons, Buddhism was again tolerated in Trans-Baikalia—though at the same time anti-religious propaganda was kept up to ensure that it did not make too much headway. This policy was continued after the war, no doubt because Stalin was concerned about his image in Buddhist east Asia; but though permission was given for one new *datsan*, the Ivolga near Ulan-Ude, to be built, and one old one, the Aga in the Chita region, to be reconstructed, severe restrictions were imposed upon the handful of lamas and novices allowed to live and practice there. The state also exerted overall control of Buddhist activities by setting up the Central Buddhist Board of the USSR, with headquarters at the Ivolga Datsan and an office in Moscow, staffed by Russians, to take care of foreign relations. The Bandido Khambo Lama, now wearing an overtly fellow-travelling complexion, meanwhile began turning up at Buddhist conferences in Asia to advocate an agit-prop sort of 'peace'. As for the St Petersburg temple, despite periodic calls for it to be put to more appropriate uses, it variously served as a trade union recreational facility, a radio contact centre for war-time aircraft, a Cold War jamming station and, latterly, as a laboratory of experimental morphology, where vivisection experiments were conducted—something particularly offensive to Buddhists.

In the relatively more liberal atmosphere that opened after the death of Stalin in 1953, two events stimulated Buddhist study and practice among European Russians. The first one was the return to the USSR of the formidable Tibetologist and Mongolist George Roerich (1902-60), the son of the famous painter, who took up a post at the Oriental Institute of the USSR Academy of Sciences in Moscow; the other was the release from captivity of the Buryat lama Bidya Dandaron (1914-74), who was not only a distinguished classical Buddhologist but a Tantric adept and guru. Though his time was short—the oppressive political climate undermined his health—Roerich initiated a revival of the great Russian tradition of academic Orientalism. Dandaron's contribution, on the other hand, was to initiate a lay tradition of Tantric practice among non-ethnic Russian Buddhists.

In all Dandaron spent some twenty-two years of his life in the Gulag, which—a reflection perhaps of his Buddhist fortitude—he regarded as particularly conducive to spiritual practice. On his second release in 1956 he obtained a post at the Buryat Institute of Social Sciences in Ulan-Ude, and soon students were gravitating to him from Moscow and St Petersburg, the Baltic States and the Ukraine. This alarmed the Communist authorities and they arrested him for a third time in 1972 on charges of organizing an illegal religious group. There were also allegations at his trial of drunken orgies, attempts to intimidate and even murder those who wished to leave the group, and financial opportunism. Dandaron was found guilty and sentenced to another term in the Gulag, while some of his students were subjected to 'ambulatory forensic psychiatric diagnosis' and temporarily incarcerated in psychiatric institutions. Unfortunately, Dandaron was no longer resilient enough to withstand the rigours and abuses to which he was subjected at the Vydrino camp —he was reputedly forced to carry on working with a broken arm and leg—and he died in 1974.

The Dandaron affair was a shock, though not a disenabling one. The small, dedicated groups of European Russian Buddhists that had formed in the 1950s and 1960s, though still illegal in the eyes of the authorities, continued to practice underground throughout the 1970s, some of them composed of Dandaron disciples—or even disciples of his disciples. In the absence of qualified teachers, they had to rely mainly on books, however, and while a few managed to persuade academic Orientalists to teach them classical Tibetan so that they could have access to basic texts, Buddhist works in Western European languages were also translated and then circulated as *samizdat* literature. A direct result of this was that Russian Buddhists were introduced to forms of Buddhism other than the traditional Gelugpa one that had been originally transmitted from Tibet via Mongolia. Zen, for instance, attracted interest through the writings of Dr D.T.Suzuki—and certain more 'popular' Buddhist ideas also infiltrated the USSR along with other Western influences during the Hippie Era.

In the freer atmosphere of Gorbachev's era of *Glasnost* the situation has improved enormously. In particular it has at last become possible for a few Buddhist groups in St Petersburg and other major centres to throw off the stigma of illegality by officially registering themselves with the authorities. In theory there is now no serious impediment as Buddhism is no longer regarded as politically contentious, but the authorities tend to drag their feet. At a meeting held at the St Petersburg temple in May 1991 to organize an umbrella organization to coordinate activities, the groups represented included the Latvian Buddhism Community of Riga, the Estonian Buddhist Community of Tallinn, the St Petersburg Religious Community of Buddhists, the Institute of Mahayana based at Tartu University in Estonia (this is led by Linnert Mäll, an Oriental scholar of repute), and the Buddhist Community of Novosibirsk, whose representative was Kungpa Nyimo, a son of Bidya Dandaron. There are also believed to be Buddhist groups in Moscow, Kiev and Kharkov, while in Tashkent, perhaps the least likely place one might expect to find one, there is a Korean Zen group. Much regeneration is under way in Trans-Baikalia too. The Tsugol and Gusinoye Ozero Datsans have been reconstructed, and there are reports of seventeen to twenty smaller Buddhist centres functioning as well. In Elista, the capital of Kalmykia, meanwhile, there is a small centre for Kalmyk Buddhists in a local house. Finally, it has now also become possible for both Asian and Western teachers and scholars to begin visiting the

USSR, which serves to break down the longstanding isolation of Soviet Buddhists.

But arguably the event of greatest symbolic significance was the return to Buddhist hands in 1991 of Kuntsechoinei Datsan, as Dorzhiev's St Petersburg temple is properly called. The new abbot there is Gelong Tenzin-Khetsun Samayev, an English-speaking lama from eastern Siberia, who was trained at the Gandan monastery in Ulan-Bator, the School of Buddhist Dialectics in Dharamsala and at Drepung monastic university in south India. He hopes to restore the temple, which like everything in St Petersburg is currently in a very depressed and dilapidated state, and to repossess its confiscated treasures. He also has plans to set up a monastic school, for he sees the small number of trained lamas as the main problem currently besetting Soviet Buddhism. Besides himself—he is in his forties—there are only seven fully qualified lamas in the whole country, and they are all over eighty years of age.

No one quite knows which way things will go, but the Venerable Samayev is optimistic. He feels that Buddhism has much to offer at a time when, due to the collapse of faith in Marxist materialism, there is an ideological and spiritual vacuum in the USSR. Certainly, its ability to rise phoenix-like from the ashes of the Stalinist holocaust has amply demonstrated the spiritual robustness of this 250-year-old tradition. The present resurgence is therefore hopefully a harbinger of greater things to come.

SELECTED SOURCES

Andreev, A. 'Iz Istorii Peterburgskogo Buddiystkogo Khrama' (On the Buddhist Temple in St Petersburg'), *Minuvshoye* (Paris), No. 9, undated offprint.

Berlin, L. 'Khambo Agvan Dorzhiev (I borbe Tibeta za Nezavicimost)' ('Khambo Agvan Dorzhiev (in relation to Tibet's Struggle for Independence')), *Novy Vostok* (Moscow), No. 3, 1923.

Bräker, H. 'Buddhism in the Soviet Union: Annihilation or Survival?', *Religion in Communist Lands*, Vol.11, No. 1, 1983.

Dorzhiev, A. *Chos. brgyad. gdon. gyis. zin. byas. te / rgyal.khams. don. med. nyul. ba. yi / dam. chos. nor. gyis. dbul. sprang. btsun, gzugs. shig. gi. bgyi. brjod. gtam*, (Autobiography), commentary by Khensur Ngawang Nima, probably Mundgod, S. India, undated (1985 or 1986 likely). A Mongolian version or variant of this text also exists.

Fenzl, F. 'Der Buddhismus in Russland in Vergangenheit und Gegenwart', *Bodhi Baum* (Vienna), 1985.

Poppe, N. 'The Buddhists of the USSR', *Religion in the USSR*, ed. B.Ivanov. Series 1, No. 59, Institute for the Study of the USSR (Munich), 1960.

Unkrig, W.A. 'Aus den letzten Jahrzehnten des Lamismus in Russland', *Zeitschrift für Buddhismus und verwandte Gebeite*, (München-Neuberg), Vol. VII, 1926.

The Inner Work of Radical Social Change
Ken Jones

A GLOBAL ECOLOGICAL CRISIS, which could cause immense suffering, has already begun to close in upon us. In order to resolve it we shall have to respond to Rosemary Ruether's question, 'How do we change the self-concept of a society from the drives towards possession, conquest and accumulation to the values of reciprocity and acceptance of mutual limitation?' [1] This implies a social revolution so radical as to require profound changes in the ways in which we relate to one another and exercise our social responsibilities. This, however, does not appear to be appreciated even by the great majority of radical Greens.

This paper argues the need, therefore, for deep *personal* change by means of an 'inner work' movement employing transformative spiritual practices, growth therapies and interpersonal skills or training.

But first it has to be said that spiritual work is ultimately about existential liberation and the transcendence of self. To see it solely as an enabler of radical social revolution would be a grotesque secular inversion. Contrariwise, it is possible to create social conditions which strongly favour spiritual work and aspiration, and that I see as being the ultimate purpose of the ecologically sustainable society envisioned here.

Even the radical Dark Greens still amount to only a tiny minority in the mass of the population, which is now turning Pale Green. No matter that the global warm-up is already set to raise sea levels sufficiently to wipe several low-lying countries off the map by mid-century. The conventional wisdom is now that we do have a serious *environmental* crisis but that this can be remedied by new technologies, global planning and 'green consumerism'. We can still have plenty of 'sustainable growth' and the business of the onward march of humanity can go on much as usual. Presumably the ultimate techfix will be the synthesizing of a biotechnical environment to replace exhausted Nature.

For radical Greens, however, the crisis is an *ecological* one which challenges deeply ingrained personal and social values. Too many of us are multiplying too rapidly, exhausting planetary resources and creating unsupportable levels of pollution. We may already have overshot Earth's carrying and self-cleansing capacities and created insoluble problems for ourselves. The notion that it is enough to identify a range of specific problems, such as acid rain, nitrate pollution or the greenhouse effect, and then develop a biotechnical solution for each, reflects a scientistic mentality which is itself part of the problem. It fails utterly to appreciate the scale, momentum, interactive complexity and problematic nature of the crisis.

As the present biotechnical crisis accelerates economically, politically and militarily an authoritarian lifeboat scenario is surely the most likely—perhaps a paternalistic technology of left or right. Surely the powerful and wealthy enclaves in the high consumption countries will endeavour to sustain as much as possible of their established lifestyle and values, whilst making the usual palliative gestures in the face of growing natural disasters, famine, disease and war. It's already familiar, isn't it?

What of the countervailing resources which history has bequeathed us? The global radical Green movement embraces libertarian Greens, socialist Greens, entrepreneurial Greens and 'New Agers'. It overlaps with feminist, peace, religious and community action movements, and with certain ethnic and national movements, to form a 'rainbow coalition'. Very broadly speaking it has inherited the romantic political idealism of Rousseau,

Godwin, Proudhon, Thoreau, Kropotkin and Tolstoy (and earlier religious radicalism).

Consider the human implications of the vision of ecotopia shared within the 'rainbow coalition'. It is a vision of confederations of culturally diverse and politically and economically autonomous nations, regions and communities, all of whose members enjoy full democratic and civil rights, personally and economically as well as politically. Their economics will be based on conservation and quality of life instead of the maximization of consumption. Their politics will be of grassroots empowerment and responsibility, with extremes of wealth and power impermissible on grounds of humanity, ecology and social stability.

In ecotopia, democratic politics would be unprecedented, in that they would not be structured, ordered and constrained by combinations of public and private corporate power, by the conditioning of the mass media or by the disciplines of the market. (Capitalism as the dominant economic system would surely be ecologically unacceptable, though I believe a humanized, small scale entrepreneurialism has much to commend it.) In short people would be left 'free' to take responsibility for themselves and one another. But how?

It is discomfiting that for the most part not even the trailblazers themselves, the radical Greens and others of the rainbow coalition, appear yet to have internalized the social values which could make ecotopia really credible. Too often their ideals are contradicted by a quarrelsome and dogmatic tone, absence of self questioning and lack of concern to really communicate even with potential allies let alone opponents.

Both the New Age end of the spectrum, and at the Green socialist end still stiff with dogmatic Marxism, the crippling symptoms of ideology are frequently present. There is the formula-writing which ingrains intellectual certitude and the emotional security that goes with it. There is the vision splendid of the New Age proclaimed by prophets and cheer leaders much as was the inevitability of proletarian revolution or the Second Coming. It's heavy stuff, as books like Marilyn Ferguson's *Aquarian Conspiracy*[2] demonstrate. And there are well defined enemies and approved outlets for gutsy feelings. The price is paid in distorted perceptions, reduced effectiveness, and lack of awareness of the inner needs which make ideological dope addictive.

It is not only a question of making a future ecotopia practicable but also of establishing credibility now. 'Every time we come up with our ecotopian vision of the future,' writes Jonathon Porritt, 'people would say, "It sounds wonderful. But to do it you're going to have to change human nature . . ." Those who choose to disregard the element of self-interest in politics —be it conventional or Green politics—are seriously deluding themselves. There is no magic carpet to some new ecotopian world. If we are to move down that road . . . we have to confront the grittiest parts of human nature.'[3]

How can we dissolve the age-old drives of oppression and exploitation, whether by gender, social class, ethnic group, by one nation and community over another, or just by simple majority? How can we engender the necessary public spiritedness, tolerance, trust and concern for co-operation and conflict resolution?

The libertarian tradition assumes that repressive institutions are what make people behave badly: power corrupts. Do away with these and natural goodness will flower. In fact, there have only been brief and problematic periods in history when 'bliss was it in that dawn . . .', and for whatever reason it has proved so far impossible to root libertarian utopias. The counter-culture of the 1960s and the New Age movement have inherited this tradition, and it does have the merit of insisting that radical social change must be founded on personal change instead of being conditioned by a social engineering elite. The political is personal. But although there has been much experiment with spirituality and consciousness transformation, the outcome has more commonly been a self-indulgent emotional regression rather than personality integration at a higher level of humanity.

A second source of hope is that 'small is (invariably) beautiful', politically, economically and ecologically. This single variable explanation of almost everything by writers like Leopold Kohr and Kirkpatrick Sale has become a Green article of faith and a substitute for creative situational thinking. Schumacher himself foresaw that this might happen when he pointed out that 'today we suffer from an almost universal idolatry of giantism. It is therefore necessary to insist on the virtue of smallness where this applies. If there were a prevailing ideology of smallness . . . one would have to try and exercise influence in the opposite direction.' He went on to complain that 'people find it most difficult to keep two seemingly opposite necessities of truth in their minds at the same time. They always clamour for a final solution. What we wish to emphasize is the *duality* of the human requirement when it comes to a question of size: there is no *single* answer. For his different purposes man needs many structures, both small ones and large ones, some exclusive and some comprehensive.'⁴

Thirdly, assuming that neither freedom nor smallness can of themselves ensure enough civic virtue, mainstream Greens seem to favour confederal regulation and control as fiscal sticks and carrots. Thus the Green Party manifesto enacts that 'the higher levels of government will be responsible for the co-ordination of the activities of the lower level councils to ensure that damaging inequalities and practices unfair to other districts do not develop'.⁵ Individual liberties would be protected by a Bill of Rights. However, thus *structurally* to protect and enhance the environment, the individual, and the different multi-tiered kinds of social collectivity from tendencies to oppressiveness and exploitation would surely require a great deal of complex legislation and regulation. And it would surely have to be backed by administrative law and justice and a burgeoning bureaucracy.

A strong concern for economic justice and equitability would compound matters further. Such a society could only be kept open and dynamic through maintaining a balance of conflicting interests, with a very high level of public spirited citizenship. And then older folk would sigh for the predictability, impersonality and even-handedness of old fashioned Weberian North European bureaucracy, slow but sure and free of nepotism and corruption. By substituting administration for politics wherever possible, that would at least leave citizens with time to learn to play the piano and grow cabbages.

Might it be that our political problems cannot be solved even by new politics—even 'personal politics'? The question is more immediate than speculation about the credibility of ecotopia. The goal is the road, and the road is as much about how we do politics as about what politics we do. And how we do politics depends on how seriously we work on ourselves. The work for people and planet needs to be in a style markedly different from conventional opinion forming, lobbying and campaigning, so that it foreshadows a different order of social values.

To pose the question at its most fundamental level, how can we act freely and yet at the same time with full responsibility for all that is other? How can we evolve towards a 'unity consciousness'?

My own starting point is a Buddhist one which is broadly compatible with a number of Western perspectives. Ultimately we act out of a profound dread or angst which stems from our sense of the transient and insubstantial nature of ourself. Life is characteristically about developing and sustaining a strong selfhood, not only through self-assertion but through a strong belongingness identity—what we belong to and what belongs to us. Moreover, this biographical endeavour is conditioned and sustained by the social institutions and values which we inherit. Both personally and historically our response to our human predicament is one of alienation and conflict, with parts of the self, with other individuals, with other social groupings and with the natural world, accompanied by a distorted, self-serving perception.

The succession of possible higher levels of consciousness has been helpfully set out by Ken Wilber in his book *No Boundary*,[6] together with a succession of growth therapies and spiritual practices whereby it is possible for a person to evolve towards 'unity consciousness'. This implies a deepening sense of inner peace, a realization that our struggle to be who we are is both futile and unnecessary, and an opening to an awareness identity unmediated by self-need which enables us to make more authentic and effective situational responses.

The spectrum of practices cited by Wilber range from relatively simple group approaches like Transactional Analysis through gestalt therapy, psychoanalysis and psychosynthesis to the spiritual training systems of the world's great religions. While it is true that some of these practices are intensive, expensive and specialized, most are more or less accessible to large numbers of people, given the necessary help of experienced facilitators and teachers and the opportunity to work in groups. For example, simple meditation and awareness practised regularly soon begins to reveal how far we shape our reality out of our own inner fears. And at the same time it slowly softens and lightens their compulsive power. It is not some movement for universal enlightenment that I have in mind, but simply the popularization of forms of inner work whereby we may all become a little more human and better able to work together.

A shift towards unity consciousness would enable us better to live out of the contradictory and paradoxical nature of social phenomena—that we are one and yet divided. Gandhi, for example, emphasized that empathy and real communication with an adversary did not imply compromise of our fundamental principles, or denial of the existence of very real conflict or refusal —to employ, for instance, strong non-violent sanctions if needs be.

In addition to the spectrum of established approaches to human growth and consciousness change mentioned above there are workshop practices designed particularly for social activists. Well known examples are Joanna Macy's Despair and Empowerment Workshops,[7] intended originally for peaceworkers, and John Seed's Councils of All Beings,[8] enabling a deeper ecological insight. Such 'empowerment' workshops are about expressing, accepting and working through fear and other negative emotions in a supportive group situation, using various techniques and rituals, and experiencing cathartic renewal for the work that has to be done. The UK Buddhist Peace Fellowship* offers workshops concerned with 'the issue of stress, conflict, tension and anxiety that affects many people actively working for the planet'. There is also a cluster of practices designed to prepare people for non-violent direct action, as well as those which have to do with conflict resolution and mediation in a wide variety of contexts. Professor Adam Curle, the BPF's President, has run mediation workshops in different parts of the UK.

If the above lie at the centre of the spectrum of inner work practices for activists, then at one end we may locate the highly developed area of interpersonal skills training. This consists of a range of techniques to enable members of all kinds of organizations to work more effectively together. Small group work is particularly well developed, but there are also methods of conference working which are more open, participative and satisfying than traditional conference procedures. (The Green Party has a special project group experimenting with new forms of discussion and decision making at party conferences.) The usual arrangement is for intensive group work with a trainer followed by much on-the-job practice. For example, a team will put aside time at the end of its formal business in order systematically to analyse how the group worked, the roles played, the hidden

---

* Now called the Network of Engaged Buddhists (NEB).

agendas, and so on. This end of the inner work spectrum is immediately interesting, 'safe' and of obvious utility and can provide an introduction to the deeper kinds of inner work. Little use of it has been made as yet in voluntary organizations.

At the opposite end of the inner work spectrum are the explicitly spiritual practices. For the secular-minded, 'spirituality' is a misleading term. For many it is at best other-worldly and socially irrelevant and at worst it opens the door to all that is socially regressive in institutionalized religion. As I understand it, spirituality in its most accessible and attractive form offers fundamental hypotheses about the human condition together with practices such as meditation to enable us to explore and experiment.

All of the foregoing suggests the need for a group which is concerned to promote inner work aimed at beneficial and non-violent social action. The group would need to be representative of the different inner work concerns and of social action movements, ranging from organizations like Friends of the Earth and Amnesty International to political groups. Its aims might be:

1. To identify, describe, systematize and publicize the various resources for inner work that already exist. I have in mind not only workshops and retreats, both free-standing and 'made-to-measure', but also ongoing assistance from consultants attached to organizations, to help develop new styles of public work, more participative decision-making, conflict resolution, small group work and the like, as well as the deeper inner work among interested organization members.
2. To monitor the above activity, identify gaps and shortcomings, and develop new resources as needs be.
3. To popularize the inner work idea so that it becomes an accepted and valued activity in the 'rainbow coalition' of social change movements.

4. To promote the formation of inner work affinity groups in various parts of the country. These could bring together like-minded people from organizations which have a similar outlook and would provide support, inspiration and guidance.

One of the tragedies of our times is the great divide between those who are struggling for a resolution of global problems exclusively in terms of policies and structures and those who have privatized themselves in the inner work. There needs to be wider awareness, firstly that the terrifying crisis in which we find ourselves has its origins in the human condition itself; secondly, that this condition is not immutable; and thirdly that it is practicable to undertake inner work which can be crucial in resolving the crisis.

REFERENCES
1. Ruether, Rosemary, *New Woman, New Earth*, New York, Seabury Press, 1975. p.205
2. Ferguson, Marilyn, *The Aquarian Conspiracy*, London, 1981.
3. In Inglis, Mary and Kramer, Sandra, eds. *the New Economic Agenda*, Forres, Findhorn, 1984. p.25
4. Schumacher, E.F., *Small is Beautiful*, London, Blond & Briggs, 1973. p.63, p.236
5. Green Party (UK), *Manifesto for a Sustainable Society*, 1987. 2.6/ AD 103.
6. Wilber, Ken, *No Boundary*, Boulder, Shambhala, 1981.
7. Macy, Joanna Rogers, *Despair and Personal Power in The Nuclear Age*, Philadelphia, New Society Publishers, 1983.
8. Seed, John, and others, *Thinking like a Mountain*, Philadelphia, New Society Publishers, 1988.

Rebirth: A Case for Buddhist Agnosticism?
Stephen Batchelor

IN 1254 THE FRANCISCAN FRIAR WILLIAM OF RUBRUCK, a missionary in Mongolia, became the first Westerner to describe a reincarnate Buddhist teacher. On May 30th that year he participated in a debate with Nestorian Christians, Buddhists and Muslims. In the report of his mission to King Louis IX of France he recounted the following episode:

> One of the wiser Nestorian priests asked whether it was possible for the souls of animals to escape after death to any place where they would not be compelled to suffer. In support of this fallacy, moreover, a boy was brought from Cataia [China], who to judge by his physical size was not three years old, yet was fully capable of rational thought: he said of himself that he was in his third incarnation, and he knew how to read and write.

Seven hundred and thirty years later, the same phenomenon was reported for the first time in the heartland of Christian Europe.

> On the February 12th 1985 in the State Hospital of Granada, Spain, Osel Hita Torres was born. He came into the world without causing his mother any pain, his eyes wide open. He didn't cry. The atmosphere in the delivery room was charged —very quiet and yet momentous. The hospital staff were unusually touched. They sensed that this was a special child.

This passage from Vicki Mackenzie's book, *Reincarnation: The Boy Lama*, describes the birth of a young boy who was shortly to be recognized by the Dalai Lama as the reincarnation of Lama

Thubten Yeshe, a charismatic teacher who had founded numerous Tibetan Buddhist centres throughout Europe, Australia and America, and had died eleven months earlier of congestive heart failure at the age of forty-nine in Los Angeles.

Following the traditional ways of determining a future rebirth, Lama Thubten Zopa, Lama Yeshe's principal disciple, began examining his dreams and consulting oracles for any signs that might indicate the whereabouts of his teacher. In one dream he beheld 'a small child with bright, penetrating eyes, crawling on the floor of a meditation room. He was male and a Westerner'. Shortly afterwards he visited Osel Ling, a meditation centre that Lama Yeshe had founded in Spain, and, lo and behold, crawling on the monastery floor was the very same child. The young boy was then subjected to a number of traditional tests to determine whether he was in fact Lama Yeshe.

> Lama Zopa sought out some of Lama Yeshe's possessions, mixed them with others of similar type and asked Osel to pick out those that were rightfully his. He started with a rosary, a fairly ordinary wooden beaded one, a favourite of Lama [Yeshe]'s, which he placed on a low table along with four others almost identical in style and one made of bright crystal beads which he thought would act as a natural red herring to a baby of fourteen months.
>
> Then, with Maria [the mother] and a few Western disciples as witnesses, he commanded Osel, 'Give me your mala [rosary] from your past life.' Osel turned his head away as if bored. Then he whipped it back again and without hesitation went straight for the correct mala, which he grabbed with both hands, raising it above his head, grinning in a triumphant victory smile.

In December, 1990, I had the opportunity to meet the five-year-old Lama Osel, as he is now known, in a Buddhist centre in Finsbury Park, London. He was a fair, attractive child, dressed in miniature Tibetan robes. For our meeting he sat cross-legged on a bed, looking down at myself and Roger Wheeler, a former student of Lama Yeshe, who were seated on the floor. After introducing ourselves, Roger said: 'I studied with Lama Yeshe and Lama Zopa at Kopan (in Nepal).'

Lama Osel eagerly replied: 'Before, I was Lama Yeshe.'

'You remember that well, do you?' I asked.

'Not all,' said Lama Osel.

'What do you remember?'

'When I was very sick they put me in the fire—I remember this piece.'

'What was it like being put in the fire?'

'Very hot. I couldn't see I was Lama Yeshe when they put me in the fire. I didn't see because I was in a stupa [a conical reliquary used for cremations]. In a photo they put me into a fire like this —I saw. In one little hole, like this, then zzp!, they put here fire. All burn. I saw in photo that it was like a monster. Eyes like this and all red.'

Although we tried, he did not respond to our further questions about his past life and talked about what he had been doing in the previous weeks and months.

What impressed me most about the young boy was the calm and dignified way in which he carried himself. Although some-times he would behave just like any other child of his age, as soon as he had to function as Lama Osel he displayed a maturity that semed far in advance of his physical age—an impression similar to that of the boy seen by William of Rubruck. That afternoon an hour-long ritual was offered by the centre for Lama Osel's long life. He was placed on a throne about six feet high, wearing a pointed Tibetan hat and saffron robes. His high child's voice led the chanting in Tibetan and he stayed completely composed to the very end without looking bored, neither fidgeting nor looking around distractedly—certainly not the kind of behaviour I would have expected from a five-year-old.

Yet being around Lama Osel raised far more questions than it answered. The basic enigma that preoccupied me as I came away was quite simply: What on earth is going on here? The most straightforward answer would have been that what was going on was precisely what was claimed to be going on: that this five-year-old Spanish boy called 'Osel' was the reincarnation of a Tibetan Lama called 'Thubten Yeshe'.

In support of this possibility is the fact that most religions assert the continuity of life after death in one form or another. In some, such as Hinduism or Buddhism, it is very specific: one is reborn in a form that corresponds to the kind of ethical or unethical actions (*karma*) that have been committed either in this or a previous life. In the monotheistic religions of the Middle East and Europe, the range of options is usually limited to either heaven or hell, which tend to be eternal. The indigenous Chinese religion of Taoism does not have such a strong sense of individual identity, but nevertheless some form of afterlife is suggested. Spiritualism, on the other hand, imagines an 'other side' from which the intact personality of this existence is able, through the agency of mediums and Ouija boards, to communicate with friends and relatives on 'this side'. Religious and spiritual traditions throughout history have explained that death is not the end of life but that some part of us, perhaps all of us, somehow carries on.

Buddhism is no exception to this. It is undeniable that the historical Buddha accepted the idea of rebirth. There are many citations in the scriptures in which he speaks in terms of rebirth and describes, sometimes in considerable detail, how actions committed in this life will determine the form of existence in a future world. When he describes the stages of sainthood, he also speaks of how one comes closer to the final goal of enlightenment in terms of how many times one must be reborn before one will be freed from the cycle of birth and death. Although there are instances in his discourses (the *Kalamasutta*, for example) where he says that the practice of Dharma is meaningful irrespective of whether you believe in an hereafter or not, the overwhelming mass of evidence does not suggest that he held such an agnostic position himself.

On the basis of such authoritative statements, Buddhists of all traditions have used the concept of rebirth not only to make sense of the process of spiritual liberation but also to provide an explanation of what carries the all-important traces of *karma* that drive the cycle of birth and death itself. An action is judged to be right, wrong, good or evil in terms of the kind of karmic consequences (*vipaka*) it will reap after death.

In addition to these views about *karma* and rebirth, Tibetan Buddhists adhere to the Mahayana doctrine of *bodhisattvas*: beings who dedicate their lives to the enlightenment not only of themselves but of all others too. As part of this doctrine is the notion that, instead of opting for the peace and liberation of Nirvana, the *bodhisattva* replaces the force of *karma* with that of *bodhicitta*, the altruistic resolve to continue taking birth as long as there are living beings in the world that need to be saved from suffering. According to Mahayana Buddhism, at any one time numerous *bodhisattvas* are taking birth wherever necessary to help other beings in whatever ways are required.

Tibetans also accept the theory and practice of Tantric Buddhism which gives detailed instruction on how to control those psychic energies and subtle levels of consciousness that are accessed through yogic disciplines. By utilizing these kinds of energy and consciousness, one can actually direct one's future rebirth to a specific place. In Tibet this form of Buddhism became the prevailing ideology of the land.

In addition to being spiritual figureheads, the lamas of Tibet also became political leaders. It was in this specific context that the Tibetans devised their ingenious and, in terms of their world-view, utterly reasonable system of spiritual heredity. As celibate monks, the lamas had no natural heirs to assume their mantles after death, but as Tantric Buddhists they could, for the benefit of others, direct their own consciousness to a suitable womb, thereby ensuring continuity of authority both within their monastery and over their political domains for many successive lifetimes. The best known examples of these are figures such as the Dalai Lama, the Panchen Lama and the Karmapa, who wielded considerable political power across the whole country. For the method to work, it presupposes that their disciples have the skills to rediscover them. This involves divination, oracular consultation, dream analysis, and so on. Only after having thoroughly tested the child and satisfied themselves that the boy (in one case the girl) is in fact the lama, will he be officially enthroned. He will then be brought up under the finest tutorial care his disciples can offer until he reaches the age of about twenty, at which time he will be reinvested with his full temporal and spiritual power. When he dies the process is repeated. Some of these lines are now in their twentieth or thirtieth incarnations.

The fact that all historical religions have tended to believe that life continues after death is not in itself convincing proof that the claim is true. Until quite recently most religions believed that the earth was flat, but such widespread belief had little effect on the shape of the planet. Appeals to evidence of this sort, no matter how emotionally comforting they may be, are far from constituting proof.

Even though the Buddha accepted the idea of rebirth, one could argue that he simply accepted the conventional Indian world view of his time. The Buddha never had to convince people that there was such a thing as rebirth. It was not a contentious issue. More or less everyone took it for granted—just as we take for granted many scientific views, which, if pressed, we would find hard to prove. It is very difficult today to put ourselves back into the frame of mind that would have existed in India six hundred years before Christ. At that time the figures of authority about the nature of the world were monks, brahmins and priests. They carried in their day as much authority as Albert Einstein or Niels Bohr carry in our modern culture. Long before the time of the Buddha, India had developed a cosmology, including the ideas of *karma*, rebirth and liberation, which was the world-view that the Buddha broadly accepted.

A curious twist here is that Westerners often find the idea of rebirth rather attractive, whereas in Buddhism it is not seen as a solution to anything but rather as part of the problem. Liberation or Nirvana means freedom from or cessation of the endless round of birth and death. Whether he really believed in it or not, the Buddha found the prevailing world view of his time quite sufficient as a basis for his ethical system. It also provided an adequate set of metaphors for his doctrine of transcendence. His main concern was not whether there is or is not life after death, but whether it is possible to live in such a way that one could transcend the whole dilemma of suffering.

I do not believe, as is sometimes claimed, that the teaching of the Buddha stands or falls on the doctrine of rebirth, and that one cannot really be a Buddhist if one does not accept it. Theologically, or should we say 'Buddhologically', it is indeed problematic to do away with the doctrine of rebirth, for numerous other basic ideas would then have to be re-thought. But if liberation is the 'taste' of the Dharma, as the Buddha said, then for its sake one should at least be prepared to put up with the unappetizing flavour of doctrinal inconsistency.

Another problem that has beset even traditional Buddhists is the question of what it is that is reborn. For religions that assert an eternal soul essentially distinct from the body/mind complex, this has never been a problem. When the body dies, the soul simply keeps going. But one of the central Buddhist doctrines (far more central than that of rebirth) is that of non-self (*anatman*), i.e. the denial of any intrinsic identity or soul or self that can either be found through analysis or mystically realized in meditation. The understanding of non-self is the key to enlightenment and liberation. It means to realize that the notion of a deep-seated personal identity, unconditioned and unaffected by anything else, is a fiction, a tragic habit into which we have become locked since, in Buddhist parlance, 'beginningless time'. In order to free oneself from suffering one needs first and foremost to free oneself from clinging to such a notion of self identity. But how does one square this with the idea of rebirth: of something distinct from that which dies but which is somehow reborn and so passes from life to life?

To answer this question, more or less every Buddhist school of philosophy has come up with a different explanation—a fact which in itself suggests that their answers are based on speculation. Most schools claim that what is reborn is some kind of consciousness. Some say that this is simply the sixth sense (*manovijnana*); others propose the existence of a foundation consciousness (*alayavijnana*); the Tantric traditions talk of a combination of extremely subtle energy and mind. But as soon as one hypothesizes the presence of some kind of subtle stuff, no matter how sophisticated the technical term one invents to denote it, one has already reintroduced the notion of some kind of self-substance. If we unflinchingly take hold of the Buddhist critique of non-self and push it to its logical conclusion, then even to cling to the idea of a subtle kind of consciousness is still a form of entrapment in reification, which is essentially in contradiction to the entire process of enlightenment and liberation.

This, I believe, is the direction in which the Madhyamaka school of Buddhist philosophy is moving, although in practice its representatives usually resist the inevitable outcome of their own logic. Having rejected all concepts of some kind of subtle substance that sneaks across from one birth to the next, the Prasangika-Madhyamikas maintain that what is reborn is the 'mere "I"'. Any further qualification will only lead one back into reification. And as for the identity of this 'I', Shantideva, an eighth century proponent of Madhayamaka, says: 'It is one person that dies and another that is reborn.' Thus *anything* that one identifies with as 'me' in this existence, no matter how subtle, will cease at death. The sheer momentum of my actions will somehow generate a form of life as different from myself now as you are different from me now. For Shantideva it is quite pointless to act out of concern for one's own welfare after death. The driving force of the ethics of *karma* is thus turned on its head: the only meaningful motive for action can be compassionate concern for others.

Several centuries after the historical Buddha, Buddhist philosophers became involved in all manner of controversies with other schools of Indian thought, some of which had a materialist outlook and denied the idea of rebirth. At this point 'proofs' were devised to convince non-believers of the truth of rebirth. These are examined with great clarity in Martin Willson's excellent little book *Rebirth and the Western Buddhist*, in which he shows that none of the arguments hold (while still insisting that the doctrine of rebirth is essential to Buddhism). The 'proofs' rest on the assumption that any moment of consciousness must be preceded by a previous moment of consciousness; that it is impossible for something material (like the brain) to produce something immaterial (like a thought). Thus one classical argument runs: 'The mind of a child that has just been conceived must have existed previously, because it is a mind.' This may convince a hypothetical Buddhist meditator who has directly experienced how consciousness in its nature arises from consciousness, but it carries little weight with a modern Westerner who is unclear whether or not consciousness is an epiphenomenon of the brain.

To proceed further along the avenue of 'proof' only leads to further problems. Let us imagine that a breakthrough in science led to the discovery of rebirth as an established fact. Many Buddhists would doubtless rejoice at this vindication of their belief. But simply to establish rebirth would in no way establish the need for any ethical linkage between one existence and the next. Just to prove that death will be followed by another life in no way indicates that a murderer will be reborn in hell whereas a saint will go to heaven. But the doctrine of rebirth is meaningful in Buddhism insofar as it provides a basis for the continuity of ethical consequences. Although rebirth and *karma* are often linked together, it is *karma* which is of primary importance; rebirth is secondary.

Likewise, even if research into the cases of young children who claim to remember their previous lives or people who recall them through hypnotic regression led to certainty about these people having been reborn, this in itself would not furnish any proof whatsoever either that they themselves would be born again or that anyone else was or will be reborn. The most such research can do is suggest the possibility of rebirth. Why, for example, could we not construct a theory of two or three lifetime-cycles (as in fact some materialist Indian schools did), after which the process would cease? To appeal to the results of such research may be consoling, but to draw the inductive conclusion that therefore rebirth is a fact of life in unwarranted.

Another kind of evidence that is often cited to 'prove' that there is life after death is that of people's reports of near-death-experiences (NDE). The problem here is that a near-death-experience is, by definition, not an experience of death. Death is not something that one returns from to talk about; rather it is the end of life; the very term 'near-death' itself makes this crucial distinction. Although NDEs might give some indications of what will happen at death, they are not reports from beyond the grave.

People who have had such experiences tend to draw extremely optimistic conclusions from them, claiming that they have now lost any fear of dying. Their whole attitude to life is sometimes completely transformed. But I wonder how much these experiences feed on a basic yearning for consolation in a post-Christian culture: a longing for a heaven that has been repudiated. A Tibetan Buddhist, for example, would have no difficulty accepting the existence of such experiences, but, given his rather different world-view, would interpret them in a far less positive way. The accounts of NDEs are similar to the descriptions of the initial stages of death in such writings as the *Tibetan Book of the Dead*. The problem is that they stop before things start turning nasty. According to the Tibetans, the initial beatific visions of radiant light and so on are, for most unenlightened people, the calm before the storm. The so-called 'Clear Light' is the point at which one touches the very ground of one's being. But once the patterns of *karma* begin to reassert themselves, one is expelled from this peaceful repose into a nightmarish series of visions that serve as the conduit to the next suffering-laced womb. In any case, many of the Tantric teachings of Tibetan Buddhism are concerned with preparing oneself to utilize the experience of death to transform fundamentally one's way of being in the world; so if a Tibetan Buddhist were to have a near-death-experience, he or she would have no difficulty in fitting it into their world-view; but it is unlikely that they would immediately draw an optimistic conclusion about life after death. At best it would reinforce their resolve to prepare themselves through Tantric practice for the Clear Light experience. It is unimaginable that such people would interpret it as an indication that death is no longer something to fear but the gateway to eternal life.

Now let us go back to the case of young Lama Osel and his predecessor. Although one hypothesis to account for how he appeared in Lama Zopa's dream and selected the right rosary would be that he is the reincarnation of Lama Thubten Yeshe, could we not conceive of an alternative hypothesis that would be no less problematic than the theory of rebirth? One has to remember that the environment in which Lama Osel has been brought up would not fulfil the criteria of strict objectivity. From a very early age he has been immersed in images of Lama Yeshe and the world of Tibetan Buddhism (like the photo he referred to in the interview), subjected to high-profile media attention because of his having been identified as a *tulku*, surrounded by people with a very high investment in believing that he is in fact the reincarnation of their teacher. Let us imagine that the child is simply responding to the expectations of the adults around him. He already knows that when he makes certain gestures or speaks in a certain tone of voice, those who care for him exclaim with joy, 'Oh, that's just like Lama Yeshe!' so when this sensitive child is confronted with a range of rosaries, could he not simply be responding to the hopes and expectations of his audience—none of whom are indifferent to the outcome? One wonders if the same tests were run under laboratory conditions in the presence of neutral observers whether the results would be the same. Whether or not one accepts such a possibility—that a young child can 'read' the expectations of those around him— is such a theory any more or less feasible than that of rebirth? As for his 'remembering' his former incarnation, it would seem quite possible to explain this in a similar way, namely that he is simply telling the adults around him what he thinks they want to hear. This is not to deny the possibility of rebirth in this case, but to show that the same phenomena can be explained by an hypothesis every bit as tentative.

So where does this leave us? Are we any clearer as to what is going on? Having looked at the traditional Buddhist account of rebirth and having reflected on some of the difficulties it presents, where does one stand? It is often felt that one has two options: one can either believe in rebirth or not believe in it. But there is a third alternative: that of agnosticism—to acknowledge in all honesty that one does not know. One does not have either to assert it or to deny it; one neither has to adopt the literal versions presented by tradition nor fall into the other extreme of believing that death is a final annihilation. This, I feel, could provide a good Buddhist 'middle way' for approaching the issue today.

Rationally, it seems impossible to know about something which presupposes that the very apparatus that does this knowing (the psycho-physical complex of my body and mind) will be absent. Whatever I say about what happens to me after death is inevitably said from the standpoint of that which will cease at death. No matter how philosophically cogent, buddhologically sound, aesthetically appealing, or psychologically astute it may be, whatever theory I propose will be limited by the senses, language, brain-activity and consciousness of a finite being (myself) who cannot conceive of anything outside the afore-mentioned senses, language, brain-activity and consciousness. The traditional Buddhist doctrine of the 'six realms of existence' (gods, titans, humans, animals, ghosts and hell-denizens), which are considered the only possible options for rebirth, betrays the necessary anthropomorphism of such a belief. All these realms (except that of the animals) are imaginative extensions of aspects of the human situation. It is impossible to imagine, for example, a seventh sense-faculty, let alone the kinds of consciousness more complex brains would make possible. Yet death, as the disintegration of the senses and the brain we now possess, surely must open up the possibility of a potentially infinite variety of forms of existence (and even the possibility of something beyond the very ideas of existence and non-existence).

Furthermore, an agnostic position towards death is more com-patible with an authentic spiritual attitude. In many cases we find ourselves drawn to doctrines such as rebirth, not out of a genuine existential insight or concern, but rather out of a need for consolation. At the level of popular religion, Buddhism, as much as any other tradition, has provided such consolation. Yet, if we take an agnostic position, we will find ourselves facing death simply as a moment of our existential encounter with life. The fundamental spiritual confrontation of human life involves the realization that we have been thrown into this world, without any choice, only to look forward to the prospect of being expelled at death. The sheer sense of bafflement and perplexity at this situation is crucial to spiritual awareness. To opt for a comforting, even a discomforting, explanation of what brought us here or what awaits us after death severely limits that very rare sense of mystery with which religion is essentially concerned. We thereby obscure with consoling man-made concepts that which terrifies and fascinates us in our depths.

True religion requires the courage to confront what it means to be human. All the pictures I entertain of heaven and hell or cycles of rebirth merely serve to replace the overwhelming and perhaps unacceptable reality of the unknown with the banality of what is known and acceptable. In this sense, to cling to the idea of rebirth, rather than treating it as a useful symbol or hypothesis, can be spiritually suffocating. If we are to take religion as an ongoing existential encounter with our life here and now, then we will only gain by releasing our grip on such notions.

REFERENCES:
Peter Jackson. *The Mission of Friar William of Rubruck.* London, 1990.
Mackenzie, Vicki. *Reincarnation: The Boy Lama.* London, 1989.
Willson, Martin. *Rebirth and the Western Buddhist.* London, 1987.

Shamans and the Ladakhi Village
Sophie Day

I. INTRODUCTION

SHAMANISM WAS EXPLORED by practitioners and commentators during a weekend conference at Sharpham in November 1988. Most of the participants were concerned with the spiritual experiences of shamans in North America and the Buddhist world. My own presentation described the ambivalence associated with 'village oracles' in Ladakh. It focused upon the public aspects of practice rather than the inner dimensions of trance. The mistrust shown towards Ladakhi oracles can be understood in several ways: below, I document just one aspect relating to the afflictions suffered by initiates.

Shamanic practice is very generally constructed out of the personal experience of affliction and madness. An individual falls ill and a novice is recognized through his or her unusual suffering, which is gradually transformed into a special healing and oracular power. As Mircea Eliade wrote:

> the shaman is not only a sick man; he is above all a sick man who has been cured. (Eliade, 1964:27)

Biographies of shamans illustrate the importance of this life history in Tibetan speaking areas as well as other parts of the world (see Brauen, 1980, for an example from Ladakh). Most accounts from Tibetan areas relate these traumatic initiations to religious experiences associated with Buddhist tantrism and/or monasticism.

Sophie Day

Eliade was one of the first widely read authorities to note the importance of shamanic experiences to Buddhism and recent accounts have developed his insights. Thus, Aziz described the reincarnate lama (*sprul sku*) as a routinized or para-shaman (Aziz, 1976) while Stablein described the master of tantric ritual as a neo-shaman (Stablein, 1976). Paul has suggested that the growing importance of monastic Buddhism among the Sherpa led to an historical shift: shamanic or possession techniques became less important in the village as they were incorporated within an expanding monastic system (Paul, 1976).

Research on shamanism in Tibetan-speaking areas has been less concerned with the village environment than with the relationship between Shamanism and (other) Buddhist practices. Similarities and differences have been pointed out in the training of ritual experts, such as monks and shamans, the associated pantheon and religious practice. In what follows, initiatory experiences are related to common afflictions in the village so as to draw attention to other relevant dimensions of Ladakhi shamanism.

2. LADAKHI VILLAGE ORACLES

Village oracles in Ladakh might be described as shamans though it should be emphasized that they do not generally travel to other worlds in trance. Instead, they become empty vessels (*lus gyar*) for gods through trance practice. These gods speak the truth about the past, present and future, and they cure visiting supplicants, primarily through the extraction of substances that have caused illness. Village oracles, like other lay specialists, are few in number and attract less respect than monks. Most ritual functions have been incorporated within the monastery. In the Leh region of central Ladakh, where I lived for sixteen months in the early 1980s, there were only a score of village oracles but many hundreds of monks.

All sorts of problems are taken to village oracles, including sickness, misfortune, theft and loss. Certain types of problems are thought to be particularly appropriate for oracular consultation. Domestic animals such as cattle and dzo (a yak-cow hybrid) are taken for treatment: 'needles' (*khab*) are extracted from their bodies. People also have substances extracted in the form of black liquid, a piece of paper or some hair. These substances are described as pollution, poison or sorcery which result from daily village sociality, notably hospitality, and occasionally the ill intentions of others.

Individuals suffering anxiety, unsettled moods or, in the extreme case, possession (*'jug-*[1]) are taken to oracles, who have suffered similar problems themselves in the past. Such problems may be taken equally to other specialists: monks, allopathic doctors, local medical specialists and astrologers. Intractable problems will eventually be taken to reincarnate lamas, most of whom live as monks, for such specialists can perform the work of all others, only better.

Symptoms of possession provide the focus for the present discussion. In Ladakh, 'possession' refers narrowly to the replacement of one's normal consciousness by some other power and broadly to a wide range of symptoms, including minor depressions and anxieties, loss of appetite, and lack of energy. These minor and common symptoms are not equated with full-blown possession; it is feared, however, that the more serious illness will develop unless appropriate preventive steps are taken. The links between minor illnesses and a dramatic loss of consciousness are asserted more often with respect to women than men. Minor symptoms in men are commonly attributed to other causes. In the Leh area, at least, possession was a very common diagnosis even though classic possession symptoms (involving loss of consciousness) seemed to be rather rare.

Oracles treat other villagers for the very problems that initiated their own careers. Oracles are elected through a possession illness

---

[1]The Ladakhi infinitive differs from the Tibetan. Only the root is given here, as in *'jug-*.

that always culminates in the classic loss of consciousness, when one or more local gods reveal their presence. An established village oracle remembers her illness and cure:

> I was very, very ill for a month. My body was so heavy that I could barely move. Yet, if I stayed at home, I'd have a fit— everything would go dark and I'd feel as if I were about to faint. Then, I'd come to with no recollection at all of what had happened. But, I didn't feel much better afterwards. I'd feel very weak and my head would hurt. I was ready to die. I was terrified. So, every day, I used to go somewhere. I'd go to Leh or to a monastery because it was so difficult to stay at home. But, sometimes, I'd have fits outside as well. I spent nearly Rs 1,200 that month on rituals, travelling and consultations. I got amulets (*srung ba*) from every monk in Leh and I visited most of the rinpoche (reincarnate lamas). At that time, there were six rinpoche in Hemis and they each gave me a blessing. But, none of them told me it was a god. I also visited the oracle, T., but he didn't tell me it was a god; he said that I would get better.
>
> One day, I visited my elder sister in Leh. It was the first time I was (fully) possessed. My sister told me that I said chod (*mchod*, a term of offering) and then the god came . . . No, I don't know what the god said. Then we realized what had happened and so the next day I went to S. but the oracle wasn't there. I went to T. but there was no one there. I went again and again to L. but grandmother oracle refused to teach me. So I went back to T. and he agreed to take me on . . .

At first, it was by no means evident what was wrong even though the loss of memory and unpredictable behaviour would have suggested possession to most Ladakhis. The novice is given all-purpose remedies, including amulets and blessings. Neither monks nor senior oracles reach a conclusive diagnosis. Symptoms persist and the goddess causing possession eventually announces herself. The novice embarks upon a specific cure and training.

Every oracle reports a unique initiation history but each history includes such episodes of 'madness' (*smyon pa*). No oracle can be authenticated without suffering a period of uncontrolled possession even if s/he is likely to have inherited the calling and the gods from relatives. About half the practising oracles in the Leh area belong to shallow 'oracle lineages' of this kind.

3. POSSESSION

The term 'possession' may refer to a wide range of symptoms; the classic loss of consciousness describes merely one end of a continuum. Possession may also result from the predations of a number of different agents, including gods, 'witches' and 'ghosts'. These are all local, worldly beings; free-floating spirits that share the village world with people or aspects of neighbours, relatives and friends. In the Leh area, the many symptoms associated with possession are attributed especially to 'witches', to the jealous projections of co-villagers who desire children, or clothes or work. In the Leh region, possession symptoms are provisionally associated with the demonic aspects of neighbours and it requires extensive negotiation to displace such suspicions.

Villagers, therefore, assume that possession symptoms have been caused by worldly beings who are, at best, amoral and, at worst, wholly sinful. The possessed attracts almost as much disapproval as the possessor. Victims were weak; they must have had low spiritual power and bad karma to allow greedy or jealous beings to penetrate their persons. Good karma, religious practice and proper conduct would have protected victims from such ill-feeling. In this way, anyone who goes mad or suffers problems that are even provisionally classed as possession symptoms reveals a personal weakness. Both agents and victims of possession attract a certain disapproval.

When future oracles fall ill, they are therefore seen as weak unfortunates who have probably been taken over by aspects of their stronger peers. Women, in particular, will be provisionally labeled 'witch victims'. Even when a god announces itself or is revealed through the divinatory techniques of ritual specialists, it is thought to be lying. The woman cited above described how she, too, was seen as the victim of witchcraft. She reported an episode at a local festival. She had dressed up in fine clothes and gold ornaments, like all the other women. Such finery attracts jealousy. The future oracle then showed classic signs of possession and everyone said that she had been taken over by 'witches'.

Months and, sometimes, years pass before the agent of possession is generally agreed to be a local god rather than a demon. Even then, the god is not sharply distinguished from ghosts or witches, for it has behaved in much the same way. It has revealed itself to be a lowly, worldly, demon-like god. Most symptoms of possession precipitate treatments that return afflicted villagers to their ordinary lives. A god-inflicted madness may elicit similar treatment, for the initiate may attempt to rid his or her person of the spirit intrusion; the god(s) may be successfully banned. Exceptionally, an individual may embrace a shamanic career and begin to transform an uncontrolled and involuntary illness associated with the demonic into a divine ritual power.

During training with senior oracles and monks, novices are strengthened so that they are no longer vulnerable to spirit intrusions. Their gods are likewise purified and settled in their vessels so that they become less and less demonic, more and more divine. The gods are also taught to speak and divine the truth for the welfare of all living beings. Oracles may acquire further skills and, over time, higher-ranking gods are often said to visit and speak through their human hosts. Such divine protectors are often acquired through religious devotions as the oracle enters meditation or makes a regular pilgrimage. Indeed, simple religious practices provide perhaps the most important route through which oracles gradually shed their links with the demonic and establish a new reputation as ritual healers.

Nonetheless, the initial affliction is never forgotten. Inaccurate prophecies, failures to cure and personal misfortunes may all suggest that the gods were not true gods and the oracle simply a sick villager who has yet to be cured:

> I was told of a Christian woman in Leh who had practised as an oracle some years previously. The god had revealed itself and the woman had begun to work without the normal training. The god's words in trance proved unreliable. Most damning was an answer that the god gave to the vessel's husband. The husband was told that his wife would never have children. The couple adopted a son but, the following year, the wife became pregnant. She stopped working as an oracle. Everyone agreed that she must have been possessed by a witch/demon (*'dre mo*).

Village shamans are forever compromised by their early afflictions and they can never dispel the frequently voiced suspicion that they are simply afflicted by capricious spirits or jealous neighbours. Moreover, aspects of trance practice serve to confirm these suspicions. It was noted earlier that oracles are called to cure possession in other villagers. They train novice oracles and exorcize spirits such as witches and ghosts. During exorcistic rituals, oracles induce states of possession in their patients. As the normal consciousness is obscured, so the visitor, usually a 'witch', appears more clearly. Oracles generally cause these visitors to be named. The humiliation of this potentially public naming is usually enough to cause the witch to go. She is sometimes also beaten out of her host.

During these rituals, onlookers are reminded once more of the similarities between gods and demons, patients and oracle-healers. Strange gestures and voices fill the room and the eyes of those entranced are rolled back so that only the whites are visible.

The similarities between possession states are as evident as the differences. The oracle looks like the patient and re-enacts a past and personal affliction in a more controlled fashion. Moreover, s/he is commonly possessed by a fierce local god who causes particularly frenzied behaviour in the vessel and who claims a particular kinship with the witches or (other) demons. At one trance, a god named witches in his client and went on to say: 'I am of your kind. I come from your family.' This was a superior spirit who could command obedience from the witches and thus cause them to leave their host. Such a god might be described as a head witch or a demonic god.

Symptoms of possession are taken to monks and doctors as well as oracles. Oracles, however, treat these symptoms in a unique fashion which demonstrates close connections with the rest of the village and with a past quasi-demonic illness. The power of oracular treatments seems to derive precisely from close involvement with the village. Problems are generally diagnosed with a wealth of detail: a particular symptom is a kind of pollution caused by relatives at a recent feast; a case of possession is due to jealousy on the part of a neighbour who has no child. Since oracular treatments involve negotiating the intimate details of a village world, it is not surprising to find that oracles maintain only a precarious distance from the ills that they diagnose. Successful oracles are among the most devout of villagers and their devotions enable them to establish an uncertain distance from the rest of the village. Such practitioners seem less susceptible to the problems of witchcraft, pollution and poison. The status of their gods has yet to be called into question.

4. CONCLUSION

Village oracles are lay ritual specialists, elected through afflictions that are similar to other common village illnesses. Oracles rank low within the overall ritual hierarchy. Many aspects of their training and practice may be understood in relation to

SHAMANS AND THE LADAKHI VILLAGE

more prestigious Buddhist techniques. Nevertheless, these brief
comments confirm the centrality of their secular village status
as well. Oracles transcend what are seen to be fundamentally
demonic attacks associated with personal weakness and related
to everyday village activities such as hospitality. Established oracles reconstruct their links with the rest of the village during
trance activities. The connections that are drawn between patient
and healer, as well as demon and god seem to be central to the
efficacy of this particular form of treatment, in contrast to the
monk's, the doctor's or the astrologer's. Oracles in trance create a
world in which they live, work and eat together with other spirits
and other people. This world is permeated with religion (*chos*)
but has little to do with Buddhist initiate practice.

REFERENCES

Aziz, B. 1976. 'Reincarnation Reconsidered: or the Reincarnate Lama
    as Shaman'. In *Spirit Possession in the Nepal Himalayas* eds.
    J. Hitchcock and R. Jones, pp.343-360. Warminster: Aris and
    Phillips.
Brauen, M. 1980. *Feste in Ladakh*. Graz: Akademische Druk-u. Verlags-
    anstalt.
Eliade, M. 1964 (1951). *Shamanism: Archaic Techniques of Ecstasy*.
    Princeton: Princeton University Press.
J. Hitchcock and R. Jones eds. 1976. *Spirit Possession in the Nepal
    Himalayas*. Warminster: Aris and Phillips.
Paul, R. 1976. 'Some Observations on Sherpa Shamanism'. In *Spirit
    Possession in the Nepal Himalayas* eds. J. Hitchcock and R.
    Jones, pp.141-151. Warminster: Aris and Phillips.
Stablein, W. 1976. 'Mahākāla the Neo-Shaman: Master of the Ritual'. In
    Spirit Possession in the Nepal Himalayas eds. J. Hitchcock and R.
    Jones, pp.361-375. Warminster: Aris and Phillips.

The Way of Replenishment
Satish Kumar

IN THE TWENTIETH CENTURY people have been madly keen to make things big; big schools, big hospitals, big businesses and big governments.

In a balanced society there should be no preference for things big. Everything should be of an appropriate size. Everything *has* its appropriate size and its appropriate place, our task is to appreciate that everything has its right size and its right place. When we put things in inappropriate places then we make problems.

There is no problem if the 'small' grass is growing on the lawn and the giant oak tree is standing up to the sky. When we want to go out and lie down on the cool grass, the oak tree is no good for us at that time, but when we want to watch the birds sitting on the tall oak tree then we want to look up at the oak tree. The grass is not too small, and the oak is not too big as long as they are in their own place.

Similarly, when we are thirsty for a cup of tea, then standing up and giving a lecture is no good. At that time, making a cup of tea is the most important act we can perform. A guest has come to our house. What is most important at that moment? Will we say, 'Oh, I am too busy doing big things, I am engaged in "big deals" like writing articles, or books or speeches.' No, all these things are unimportant at that moment. A guest has arrived in our kitchen and the most important thing we can do at that moment is to make a beautiful cup of tea for our guest. In Japan, the making of tea has been elevated to ceremony and it is not a small or a menial task.

When we realize that every action in our life is as important as any other action, then our life becomes much more balanced. If we say, 'Why do I have to cook dinner, why do I have to do the washing-up? I have many more important things to do, why doesn't my wife or my husband do it, or why doesn't my daughter do it, or why can't I get some help in the house?' then our heart is not in the cooking and therefore the cooking becomes a chore, a burden. When our heart is in the cooking then it becomes a ceremony, a celebration.

In Indian tradition all food is cooked for the gods and always offered first to the gods and then to the family, to friends and guests. The cook is not even allowed to taste the food while cooking: whether the rice, the potatoes or vegetables are cooked or not, whether there is enough salt or spice, all this we learn to know by intuition, by our presence, by our total and complete awareness of the action we are performing.

We are not to do ten things at the same time. If we are listening to the radio and cooking, watching TV and cooking, answering the telephone and cooking, then it is not a sacred celebration, it is not cooking which can be offered to the gods. It is only when we have total and complete awareness of cooking that it becomes a spiritual act.

The lives of people in these days, have become artless, heartless and monotonous. Doctors, lawyers, accountants, engineers, drivers, whatever we are, our heart is not in our work. Quite often people are working only to pay the bills. Is that the meaning and purpose of our lives? Where is the real work? If the real work is not in the kitchen, if it is not in the office, if it is not in the workplace, if it is not in the garden, then where is it? And when do we do our real work? If our real work cannot be done today then when will it be done? Real work cannot wait to be done tomorrow, it cannot wait to be done when we retire, it cannot wait till we go to church, it cannot wait till we make a pilgrimage. Every moment of our life is our real work and every action we do, should be for the realization of God.

There are three dimensions to real work. The first relates to the earth, to the soil, to the environment, to nature. The second relates to society and to the people around us. The third relates to our soul and to our self-realization. In the Indian tradition the first is called *Yagnya*, the second is *Dana* and the third is *Tapas*.

Let us start with our relationship to nature and the environment, because the environment is threatened and needs our proper attention.

We come from the earth and we are made of the earth. If we did not eat the fruits of the earth we would not be able to survive. Every day we drink water which comes from the earth, our foods and forests come from the earth. Our houses, bricks, stones, slates, wood, mud, steel, have come from the earth. Everything which keeps us warm—oil, coal or gas—has come from the earth. If we go on using the earth uncaringly and without replenishing it then we are just greedy consumers.

We should take from the earth only what are our absolute and basic necessities; things without which we cannot survive. Earth has an abundance of everything, but our share in it is only what we really need.

There is a story to illustrate this. Mahatma Gandhi was staying with the first Indian Prime Minister, Mr Nehru, in the city of Allahabad. In the morning Gandhi was washing his face and his hands. Mr Nehru was pouring water from the jug as they talked about the problems of India. As they were deeply engaged in serious discussion, Gandhi forgot that he was washing. Then something happened: before he had finished washing his face, the jug became empty. So Mr Nehru said, 'Wait a minute and I will fetch another jug of water for you.' Gandhi said, 'What! You mean I have used all that jugful of water without finishing washing my face? How wasteful of me! I use only one jug of water every morning.' He stopped talking, tears flowed from his eyes. Mr Nehru was shocked. 'Why are you crying, what has happened, why are you worried about the water? In my city of Allahabad there are three great rivers, the Ganges, the Jumna and the Saraswati, you don't need to worry about water here!' Gandhi said, 'Nehru, you are right, you have three great rivers in your town, but my share in those rivers is only one jug of water a morning and no more.'

Now, that was an example of ecological thought, of conservation of resources, of replenishment. What do *we* do? Leave the tap on! Waste is the curse of our civilization. In cities like New York or London there are mountains of waste. Factories go on producing and producing. Whether our society needs these products or not does not matter, we have to keep the boys in jobs. That is why work has become oppressive, boring and heartless. There is no meaning in that work. We are producing things we don't need. We make them, take them and throw them away.

Nobody is going to be so wise to make me a Prime Minister! But if for twenty-four hours I was given the chance I would introduce one simple, earth-friendly law which would require every manufacturer to make all packaging returnable and reusable. Britain is perhaps the only country where milk is still delivered in returnable bottles. But even here Coca-Cola, wines, whiskies, fruit juices and hundreds of other items are packed in throw-away packaging. Bottle banks are no true answer. Every bottle, like the milk bottles, should be returned and reused. We have been so blinded by our addiction to convenience that we let ourselves be the cause of our own bleak future.

There is plenty in this world for everyone's needs. There is no shortage. We put one seed in the ground and we get a big tree which gives fruit year after year, so much fruit that we cannot even count it. If we plant one apple tree, how many apples do we get? There is enough for everyone's need, but not for anyone's greed. We have to return to our basic needs which are simple and the earth can fulfil them. Our real needs are not just physical, they are emotional, they are spiritual, they are intellectual, they are cultural. In fulfilling these non-physical needs there will be no depletion of the earth's resources.

One of the most fundamental of human needs is for love. Is there any lack of love in this world? No. The more we give, the more there is; and yet we are reluctant to give or to receive. We are often frightened and suspicious of each other. If somebody hugs us, we wonder why, what is the matter, what have we done? We have truly forgotten how to give and how to receive love.

Similarly there will be no depletion of resources in fulfilling our creative needs. Therefore let us make poetry, let us sing, let us dance and let us find more time for joy and for celebration so that our real needs are met. We seem to think that by having more cars, houses, clothes, furniture, we might become satisfied and happy. Yet discontent is all around us. What is the cure for this discontent? Not more things. If more things were able to make people happy Western society would be very happy!

Our first thought should be to limit what we take from the earth, our second thought should be to make good what we have taken. For example a caring gardener puts compost on the soil to restore its fertility. Once I was talking to the late Lady Eve Balfour who said, 'I look after the soil. If the soil is in good heart the plants will take care of themselves.' Soil erosion is taking place all the time. People put more chemicals into the soil so that they can get bigger crops, and bigger vegetables. Lady Eve said, 'You don't need to worry about bigger plants, worry about the soil.'

Another example is the Buddhist tradition in which every person has the religious responsibility to plant trees. The Buddhist emperor Ashoka advocated that every Indian citizen should plant five trees and look after them.

Richard St George wrote an article in *Resurgence* saying that a tree should be planted to mark the birth of a child, a Birthday tree, like we have a Christmas tree. What a splendid idea! We

Satish Kumar

can plant a tree on our birthday or even better, plant a tree on every birthday.

If we use one tree and plant another tree that is replacement, but if we use one tree and plant five trees that is replenishment. The practice we need to cultivate is to replenish the earth every day. We take from the earth every day so we should give back every day. It is a kind of 'debt' we owe to Mother Earth and we have to pay our debt. If you have a debt to the bank, the Manager writes you a letter. Mother Earth cannot write a letter, so we have to remember ourselves. Only by replenishing the earth will we keep the Earth Bank in business, otherwise it will go bankrupt. Our actions to replenish the earth are called *Yagnya*.

Then comes *Dana*: the replenishment of society. We owe a debt to our ancestors, to great religious figures like Jesus Christ and the Buddha. We owe a debt to the American Indians and the Bushmen of the Kalahari. We owe a debt to our teachers, to our mothers, fathers, sisters, brothers, husbands and wives. How much they have done for us! We owe a debt to great authors like Tolstoy, Dostoevsky and Shakespeare. Just as we take from past generations so we must give something back for future generations. That giving is *Dana*. Mother Teresa's work in Calcutta is *Dana*. It is not only giving gifts at Christmas time, but the gifts of every day. All our work is a gift to society; earning money is a by-product. We are not born into this society to pay the bills! We are working to make a gift, to enrich and to replenish society. Our work has deep meaning—it should be an act of worship, a form of art, a way of self-fulfilment.

The poetry of Goethe and Milton, the myths of *Ramayana* and King Arthur, the paintings of Van Gogh and Turner, the Pyramids, the Taj Mahal and thousands of other achievements of the past are the true capital we have inherited. Like in a family business, if we live only on the capital and do not replenish it, eventually all the capital will come to an end. It is good to cherish and enjoy the fruits of our heritage but it is also important to add our contribution to it. That is why we are required to write a poem, paint a picture, build a beautiful house; not merely to earn a living but to replenish the culture and the society.

While we are paying our debt to the earth and to society we also have to replenish ourselves. There is a lot of wear and tear on our soul. Souls are wounded every day, sometimes by anger, sometimes by lust and greed, or sometimes by anxiety and fearfulness. There are all kinds of forces making our souls sick. Unless we are able to heal our souls we cannot be whole. Neither can we replenish society and the earth. So by meditation, by fasting, by going for a walk, sitting by flowing water, by gazing at a flower, by going on a pilgrimage or a retreat, by studying the scriptures which inspire us, we are working towards our own replenishment. If we ourselves are not happy we cannot make anyone else happy.

Our society is obsessed with material growth. How much more do we need? There is no end to it. If we do not know when enough is enough, there will never be enough. But the moment we know that enough is enough we will realize that we already have enough. It is time to say 'enough' to material growth and possessions, so that our energy, our attention, our time, can be devoted to something deeper, something more meaningful, something spiritual. But we have no time, our diaries are full up. We are too busy. This is not a good situation; we should always have time for *tapas*. When God made time, he made plenty of it, we have measured it into days and hours and we have squeezed it into diaries, calendars and appointments.

There is a story in *Ramayana*: a giant called Khumbhakarna was hyperactive, so his mother said to the gods, 'My child is too active. He can do everything in half the time and therefore when he has nothing useful to do he becomes destructive.' So the gods gave the mother a boon, 'Your son will be awake for only six months and when he goes to sleep he will remain asleep for six months.' The western industrial work force is like that giant.

Because of modern technology essential needs can be fulfilled in half the time, but instead of using the rest of the time for spiritual and cultural pursuits we go on producing unnecessary and wasteful goods which are destructive not only to our souls but also to the earth. I think it would be very good if Western people went on holiday or to sleep for six months and did only what was necessary in half the time!

Our problem is that we don't sleep enough. We watch television in the night when we should be sleeping and we get up early so that we can commute two hours to London or wherever. Lots of people commute for hours every day. So people are tired, exhausted and busy. We have lost our common sense; we don't sleep well, we don't eat well and we work too much. In our sleep we can have beautiful dreams, when we are sleeping we are not inactive. Dreaming is a subtle activity. If we do not allow ourselves some time to dream then what is life worth living for? Dreams replenish the soul.

The Emperor of Persia once asked his Sufi teacher, 'Tell me what is the most important thing for me to do?' After some thought, the teacher said, 'My Lord, I would suggest that you sleep as long as you can.' 'What! What is this advice? I have to do so much work, I have to dispense justice, I have to make laws, I have to look after my people.'

'My Lord, the longer you sleep, the less time you will have to oppress.' How about giving this advice to our Prime Ministers and Presidents?

Personal Identity in Tantric Practice
James Low

I WANT TO TAKE THIS OPPORTUNITY to record some of the experiences and dilemmas that have arisen whilst engaging in tantric practice. I will not give much background information regarding the formal details of the practice as that is available elsewhere.* Rather, I will write personally about how it actually feels to be engaged in tantric practice through time and then look at a Western model of change that has been useful to me in making sense of my experience.

I started Tibetan Buddhist tantric meditation in 1973. Previously I had meditated for some two years according to a Hindu system. I was living in India at the time and meditation seemed very natural—part of acceptable, normal behaviour. I had in fact been in India several times and always with a sense of searching for something. I found great relief in the mess and chaos. It gave me freedom to relax and gradually shed the Protestant work ethic imbibed during my Scottish childhood. There seemed to be space for my own confusion and unformed longing. At the time it felt as if I was being propelled towards something, though now, reflecting on those years, I have much more sense that I was equally running away from something. The conflicts I had at home, at university, in relationships and in myself could be ignored and transformed into an impetus for this spiritual quest I was undertaking. As a renegade social anthropologist I had abandoned participant observation in favour of cultural baptism by total immersion.

---

* See references at end of article.

The one important thing that I found in Tibetan Buddhism was the notion of certainty: the idea that there is an absolute reality that can actually be known, and not only known about from afar but known as the very essence of one's being. The fact that this belief was being propounded by people who were themselves displaced made it especially acceptable. Refugees, living in camps, often in great poverty—the ordinary Tibetans as well as the lamas—seemed to have an unshakeable optimism and a sense that social identity was not terribly important. For an alienated 1960s social drop-out this was very reassuring, and indeed I read the lives of the great Tibetan religious heroes like Padmasambhava and Milarepa as a vindication of social peripherality.

I was on the edge and in my perception Tibetan teachers were also on the edge. The focus was on future lives, improved rebirths and future realization. The preparation for becoming truly centred and grounded seemed to involve a great deal of social distancing and personal destabilization. Traditional texts and teachings are rather formal, coming across as statements of how things are. In the Nyingma tradition the practices and their commentaries are factual, descriptive and elaborative. They do not go in for discussion and comparison, for they are designed to instruct not to furnish the reader with interesting ideas to develop conceptually. This style has the advantage of simplicity and clarity, but its very starkness also seems to invite personalization. Coming from a Western academic background, I was accustomed to developing meaning by juxtaposing ideas, letting books talk to each other in my mind so that new insights could occur. And, naturally enough, I applied this to the Tibetan teaching as a means of deriving a meaning that connected with my existing cognitive material.

It is one of the basic paradoxes that in order to receive the teachings one must be a pure vessel, a *tabula rasa*, free of defiling habits of interpretation. But then, to apply the teachings, one has

to have knowledge of oneself and be in touch with all the preju-
dices and knowledge upon which one's ordinary life is based.
Trapped within this, I, largely unconsciously, adapted the teaching so that it fitted my own predispositions and came to reflect
back my own alienated sense of the world. Instead of adapting to
the Dharma, I was understanding it in a way that reaffirmed my
own position on many things.

As an example of this I want now to focus on a particular
practice that I have employed for many years. As is well known,
taking refuge in the Three Jewels is the basic act or attitude
that distinguishes Buddhists from non-Buddhists. In addition to
providing personal containment and orientation, taking refuge
in the tradition also means not having to expose personal insecurity. For one can learn and use the language of the system, the
'Dharma-speak' of technical terms and foreign words that helps
to defend one against the pain and confusion of the struggle for
felt, direct knowledge. I feel quite anxious about removing this
familiar, comforting screen—anxious at the degree of confusion
to which it will expose both myself and others. In order to avoid
the defence and also not to feel too exposed, I will write in a very
loose, personal way and not attempt to tidy up any inconsistencies or make too much sense of it. In this way I can provide myself
with a future defence of denial should I feel I need it!

The practice that concerns me here is that of the *yidam*, the
deity to which the mind becomes bonded. The *yidam* I have used
is a wrathful form of Padmasambhava. I have done the practice
for about twelve years, sometimes intensively and sometimes in a
rather nominal way. The *yidam* is described as being the bestower
of attainments: the realized being who gives the actual experience of the inseparability of form and emptiness (*shunyata*).
There are two aspects to the *yidam*: (1) the aspect that can
be developed by one's efforts following the connection created
during the initiation, and (2) the natural aspect which descends
from its pure realm and fuses with the intentionally developed

aspect. The first is the 'bond aspect', the mode that represents
the potentiality generated during initiation, while the second is
the wisdom aspect, the mode that blesses the bond aspect and
transforms intention into actuality.

The practice itself can be done in long or short form, the short
taking about twenty minutes while the long requires four to five
hours. Whichever form is used, the essential point is to let go of
one's ordinary identity and enter into the identity of the *yidam*.
The practice I use belongs to Anu Yoga and so the focus is on
experiencing the felt presence of the *yidam* rather than on the
precise visualization of the form in all its details. The adoption
of the new identity is done in an instant, like a fish turning in a
stream. There is no need of any transition since the bond-aspect
and the wisdom-aspect arise simultaneously. At the end of the
formal sitting practice the presence of the *yidam* is experienced
in all the aspects of the outside world. Everything becomes this
divine reality. And each new session of sitting meditation is like
a booster injection to the ongoing reality of the presence of the
yidam both as one's own form and as the experience of the world
and its inhabitants.

Presented in this way, there is a sense of gain, of the opening
up of a new dimension of light and clarity, a continuum of
awareness. This is what the text, the teaching and the tradition
point towards, and in many ways it is absolutely true. However,
in my experience, there is also a shadow side of loss that is
not addressed in the tradition. The wish to be free of solely
Samsaric experience is a basic Buddhist attitude. The urge is
towards Enlightenment, which may be seen as something quite
other, or as a state which can both integrate and transcend Sam-
sara, the world of form. In either case, the focus is on attaining
something new, though original, which is better than ordinary
reality. However, my ordinary sense of myself, of being James,
is part and parcel of my experience of the ordinary Samsaric
world of people and places and things. I am attached to being

James and, until now at least, no amount of trying to be the deity completely releases me from the sense of loss at abandoning being James. This attachment to being James does not manifest directly except as a restraint to actually doing the practice. If I think about it then, yes, I am convinced, both by the philosophy and by my own experience, that there is a truer mode of being than the ego conglomerate described by the term 'James'. The effects of the deeply rooted attachment to an ordinary Samsaric identity is experienced primarily in a disguised form as the affect of deep loneliness and absolute alienation that comes from time to time during my practice of the *yidam*. The clarity and luminosity of the presence of the *yidam* becomes overshadowed by a sense of being lost. Here I am in the midst of this cosmic vastness, all alone, wrapped in flames, dancing and roaring in the flow of destruction of all that is reified, substantial, familiar. What utter alienation and abandonment! All the loss of all that is familiar engulfs me . . . I can't retreat and can't progress. Where am I?

The following lines by John Clare (1793-1864) give a sense of what I feel:

Written in Northampton County Asylum

I am! yet what I am who cares, or knows?
My friends forsake me like a memory lost.
I am the self-consumer of my woes;
They rise and vanish, an oblivious host,
Shadows of life, whose very soul is lost.
And yet I am—I live—though I am toss'd

Into the nothingness of scorn and noise,
Into the living sea of waking dream,
Where there is neither sense of life, nor joys,
But the huge ship-wreck of my own esteem
And all that's dear. Even those I loved the best
Are strange—nay, they are stranger than the rest.

Indeed it does feel like a kind of madness, a self-induced psychosis in which I seem to inhabit a parallel dimension, a limbo encompassing both heaven and hell. The Dharma response to such an experience is generally to see it as an obstacle—something to be worked through with faith in the ultimate value of the practice. Doubt is seen as error—and there is no place for any concept of the Dark Night of the Soul.

Well, in a sense, so be it. Having taken the initiation and entered the practice I am committed to go forward and, as part of my total practice, to make use of the *yidam*. But I also need a way of re-framing my actual experience so as not to get trapped in depressed and self-pitying perceptions.

The Western model that I have to use in trying to make sense of my experience is that of Van Gennep's concept of the rite of passage. In this, he distinguishes three phases in the transition from one social state to another. The first phase is *separation*, which (to quote Turner, p.24) 'clearly demarcates sacred space and time from profane or secular space and time . . .' It includes symbolic behaviour, especially symbols of the reversal or inversion of things, relationships and processes secular —which represents the detachment of the ritual subjects (novices, candidates, neophytes, or 'initiates') from their previous social statuses. The second phase is *transition* and in it, 'the ritual subjects pass through a period and area of ambiguity, a sort of social limbo which has few (though sometimes these are the most crucial) of the attributes of either the preceding or subsequent profane social statuses or cultural states.' The third phase is *incorporation* and it 'includes symbolic phenomena and actions which represent the return of the subject to their new, relatively stable, well-defined position in the total society.'

My experience of being lost in a limbo is an effect of both the anxiety of the separation phase and the ambiguity of the transition phase. Neither caterpillar nor butterfly, I inhabit a twilight zone of semi-identity composed of aspects of both past and future modes.

Well, is this all just fantasy? An indulgence of my emotions when I could be better served in working them through in the practice itself? Maybe so, and yet somehow the question of personal identity cannot be denied. For if I am walking about outwardly James but inwardly experiencing myself as something quite different, am I not guilty of bad faith with those I meet? Am I not turning social interaction into a charade? My work is with people. I do not live in a cave but in a city. There is tremendous pressure to retreat from the transition and separation phases and just be normal, doing my job, passing the time. It almost seems as if I'm damned if I do and damned if I don't.

It seems to me that at this time the Dharma is practised in two ways. The first is with the traditional view of the infinity of time and the endurance of consciousness. The practice of the Dharma is that which releases one from being trapped in becoming. The second attitude is to perceive the Dharma as a means of life-enhancement—a way of making one more able to cope with this present life. The second view turns the Dharma on to one's life, adapting it to fit individual needs, while the first is about adapting one's life to the Dharma and letting go of all that doesn't fit in. Commencing my Dharma practice in India, I have been much influenced by the more traditional first view and this no doubt reinforces the kind of experience I have been describing.

One of the things that strikes me is that the tantric path of transformation affirms duality in a subtle way. As a path involving intention and effort it focuses on transforming limitation into Enlightenment. And although I conceptually understand the teachings about the nature of the transformational deity (*yidam*), I find I project all sorts of parental, saviour feelings on to the *yidam* which further increase the duality and inhibit my own possibility of attainment. Devotion is a strong urge in everyone and, given that my sense of self-esteem is often low, I easily get hooked into worship rather than practice.

Out of this confusion, I have found relief in the focus of Dzogchen (lit. 'The Great Perfection', said to be the highest teaching in the Nyingma tradition), which starts with the basic knowledge of one's own nature. Without that knowledge meditation is said to be of little value as it remains within the relative dimension. This is certainly my experience. In trying to understand the Dharma and the nature of the deity I lost all sense of myself. Now I concentrate on trying to observe myself and understand the working of my mind so that I will be able to recognize its habitual responses and remain in the presence of the natural state.

For as Polonius said in *Hamlet* (I.III):

> This above all: to thine own self be true;
> And it must follow, as the night the day,
> Thou canst not then be false to any man.

Rather than adapting myself to the Dharma or the Dharma to myself, I want to understand myself in both absolute and relative dimensions. I had earlier taken the Buddhist view of 'no-self' to indicate the abandoning of relative identity for identity with a deity. After much struggle, I find these grand aspirations unhelpful. In response to John Clare's plea 'I am! yet what I am who cares, or knows?'—now at least I know where to start looking for the answer, and it is not to be found in the words of others.

REFERENCES

Beyer, S., *The Cult of Tara*. Berkeley, University of California Press, 1973.
Gennep, A. van, *The Rites of Passage*. London, Routledge and Kegan Paul, 1950. (First published 1908)
Guenther, H.V., *The Tantric View of Life*, Berkeley, Shambhala, 1972.
Lama, C.R. and Low, J., *sGrub 'Khor rNam-gSum*. Translation with Tibetan text. Shantiniketan, Chimmed Rigdzin Society, 1975/6.
Turner, V., *From Ritual to Theatre*, New York, Paj Publications, 1982.

Farewell Discourse at Sharpham
Ajahn Kittisaro

THE END OF MY TIME as senior monk at the Devon Vihara has come and very soon I shall be going back to Amaravati, the main monastery in Hertfordshire. I've been coming to Sharpham for about four years now and again I'm honoured to have this occasion to speak about the teachings of the Buddha. I think the main feeling that I have is one of gratitude for having encountered such a teaching and also for having the opportunity to live a life in which I so often meet virtuous and reflective people. I have been encouraged so much by my experience of people down here in the South West gathering together to question, to inquire into what are we doing with our lives, what is worth doing, who we are, is what we have been creating worth continuing.

I've also had the chance to lead many weekend retreats and give many informal talks, which has given me an opportunity to get to know many of you, and I wish you all to persevere with your own efforts to see through the maze of beguiling experiences with which life presents us. There is this tendency that we all feel to identify with what we are experiencing. We take our perceptions—what we see, hear, feel and so on—and become those perceptions. We become someone who is young and misunderstood by his family and someone who is old and feel they are over the hill; or we become British or American or meditators; or we become virtuous people or sinners, hopeless cases, people on the verge of breakthroughs who've blown it and don't have the guts to go through with it any more . . . This is an incredible capacity we have to create a world of beings and to identify with the little niche that appears through our thoughts.

But many of us get a sense that we're not doing it right—that there's something other than just reacting to life, just blaming and being caught up in anguish and anxiety and despair. We then encounter a teaching that holds up the notion of freedom and understanding, the possibility of living in perfect harmony with how things are, the idea of deathlessness, of the unshakeability of the heart. These are all very high-minded thoughts and there is something in us that feels almost the opposite of them. As egotistical entities we don't feel the deathless; we feel incredibly vulnerable and mortal. But that notion of the possibility of freedom—that's the beginning of the religious life, of that longing to come home to some sense of resolution and completion. Unfortunately, we sometimes linger with pleasantly consoling thoughts about deliverance and transcendence, eternity and immortality, and are content with that. It then becomes just another form of pain killer, really. It just diverts us from asking why we experience this sense of birth and death or confusion. Hence in the great religious traditions we don't stop with the notion of transcendence but we practise the way to the realization of that truth; that is, we cultivate skilful means that enable us to make contact with the world in which we live in order to understand it.

This is what religion is meant to be. The word derives from the Latin *religio*: 'to bind back'. Now bindings can imprison us. We can be bound by some kind of relationship in which we feel trapped, or by some sort of conditioning by which we feel smothered, or by an oppressive government. But these are not the kind of bindings 'religio' refers to, for we can also consciously accept a limitation. We can consciously give ourselves to staying with something rather than endlessly running, avoiding, rejecting. Ironically, this sort of binding can be very liberating because it gives us the opportunity of understanding limitation and so of transcending it.

Among the practical limitations that the great traditions, like the Buddhist one, offer to us as a foundation for clear-seeing is the limitation of virtue. Rather than identifying with and impulsively becoming everything that we think and feel, we begin to say, 'No, I won't say that . . . I won't do that . . . I won't act on impulses to harm, exploit, cheat, deceive . . .' In the Buddhist tradition these are formalized as the Five Moral Guidelines (or Precepts). They aren't sent down from above but are generated from our own intentions: the heart aspires to go beyond being impulsive, it is tired of being enslaved by anger and the destruction, remorse and confusion that come from it. Tired too of thinking that just by accumulating material things we can somehow stave off insecurity and the feeling of vulnerability. Something in us senses that this doesn't work. Many of us in this room have many different *things*, and yet we still experience frustration, anxiety, sadness, confusion.

The first limitations that we can consciously undertake is of intending our minds to harmlessness and to inquiry rather than just following what this voice inside says I want to do. We are beginning here to question the 'I want'. We are not obliterating those feelings, or telling ourselves we shouldn't have them; we're merely choosing not to follow them so that we can look at them. We can then feel what desire is. From the moment that we start to do this, even though we are limiting ourselves and there is the sense perhaps of being imprisoned, there is also ironically a beginning of a real relationship with our environment.

So, when we avow not to kill; not to take that which is not given; not to follow improper sexuality (in other words, get a perspective on our passions, not feeling that we have to follo v them all the time); not to speak deceitfully, harshly or divisively but to use language to inquire, encourage, harmonize, point out, warn; not to avoid reality by getting drunk but to cultivate the courage to be with conditions so that we can see their nature—this kind of practice gives us a connection with everything around us. When we are harmless, moreover, every creature around us can breathe easier; every person with property, every person who has a sense of relationship with something can be more at ease because we are not feeding greed.

The modern notion of what religion is about is often so grasping and materialistic. I selfishly want to take myself to eternity, to be delivered to some kind of land where I just get everything I want. So often this is what we ask God for, or want from Buddhist practice. I don't know about you but I see this tendency in myself. This kind of practice inevitably ends in disappointment and despair.

I remember a year ago several of we monks and *anagarikas* from the Devon Vihara were on our way to our main monastery, and we happened to be going by Stonehenge right before dawn at the winter solstice. We didn't plan it but, of course, someone remembered and then something in the mind went, 'Oh, this could be a big one! A very holy sign.' It still wasn't dawn yet; we got out of the car and noticed that the police were allowing people to go right up to the stones. There was already quite a bizarre gathering of beings—of course, I was perfectly normal! —all kinds of people in different sorts of robes, different kinds of music going on, little fires were being lit. It all seemed to be orientated a certain way, so I kind of figured, 'Ah, they're waiting for the sun to come up.' I was checking out my consciousness, you know, feeling everything, looking at these big rocks—there must be something here!—and we kept waiting and waiting. And there was this nagging doubt, 'Has it happened yet?'. Some of us said, 'You know, I think the sun has risen', and someone else said, 'No, no it hasn't come up. That's pre-dawn light there.'

Then I had to go to the loo and, finally, the urgency was too much, so, as the senior monk, I decided, 'It's happened'. We then started walking away past the policemen, and trying to find some sort of loo. Immediately it became dire emergency because I was in bad shape. We finally noticed there was a portable loo and I rushed into it—*and they'd turned the water off!*—but, anyway, I decided not to worry about the water. A few minutes later, as we walked to where the car was parked, I suddenly saw this magnificent ball of fire was half way up the horizon. I thought, 'Oh no, I've missed it—but maybe I only missed half of it . . . !' And then the humour and beauty and perfection of it all came to me. I mean, why do we make these sorts of moments special and sacred, and make others the orphans and lepers of our consciousness. Sacrilege means to steal away the sacred. And here lies death too.

My first encounter with religion was through meditation. I didn't actually know what I was doing at the time. I just realized that if I sat down and kind of revved up, something started to happen: I started to see lights and things.

I thought, 'That must be something. The word "enlighten-ment" has light in it.'

So I went off to my first temple in London. Well, I was hungry, so I brought a sandwich into the big hall. The people there got infuriated that I had profaned the temple by doing this gross worldly thing of eating in it. That was sacrilegious in their eyes. I didn't know it was wrong. In those days I was rather insensitive, opinionated and arrogant.

As soon as we attach to some idea of what is truly holy, then at that moment we have bowed before an idol: the idol of views. Those are the really tricky idols, the ones that are hard to see. When I first saw those lights in my meditation, thirteen or fourteen years ago, I was going around as someone who was having visions. Then, when I got to the temple, I was someone carrying sandwiches into a holy place and they were telling me that I couldn't talk to the Mahatma until I had done a number of hours service, so I was going about being outraged. Then, when I said, 'You tell me I can't be experiencing this stuff! I am experiencing this stuff! I want to talk to somebody', I wasn't someone who had seen the light any more but someone who was misunderstood. Then I was someone who was going around looking for a teacher. And sometimes we can even be someone who has found the way. But all these things are dead, because they are based on grasping at what is really just a bubble.

When we grasp at something, imagining it to be real, solid, when we make an assumption about that, then, when things really change, as they inevitably will, we have the experience of death. Also, when we've assumed health and we get sick, there is a tremendous sense of something being wrong. And when we assume a solidity to our loving relationships and to their objects, then, when we are parted from them, there is again despair. Also, when we assume a kind of security in confident thoughts, then, when doubt emerges into consciousness, there is great confusion.

Now, the Buddha used the word 'ignorance' to describe this tendency to grasp and to try to make a solid sense of self out of the bubbles of change. When there is not clear-seeing then there is the tendency to identify; and when we identify and things change there is the tendency to death and all the confusion and fear that surround it; and where there is death there is the tendency for the heart to be re-born. We can explore this if we're interested. In the period of silent meditation we've just had, I hope we had the opportunity to notice how we die and are re-born, what the mind is gravitating to, what the heart is staving off from fear—or just the restlessness or whatever. Just to begin to see these things is insight meditation: seeing into the nature of things. And when there's seeing into the nature of things then there's the opportunity to begin to be humble and learn from the orphans of consciousness and to attend to the lepers of our heart. Then we begin to be open to the possibility that the sacred is always *here* and *now* rather than limiting it to winter solstices at Stonehenge, or to sitting on the meditation cushion, or being with our beloved, or when we're seeing lights and having visions.

The Buddha would say that the truth is *akaliko*: not bound by time or place. Wherever we are, whatever we're doing there, it's there. In fact we're immersed in truth, swimming in it, but we don't necessarily see it if we are grasping at the opinion that it's somewhere else, or that we have to be someone else, or do something else. Rather than telling us that we have to change the Buddha offers a reflection, a reminder to the heart to be open and sensitive to how it is now. Then there's *ehipassiko*; *ehi* means 'come' anu *passiko* means 'look'. The truth is actually inviting us if we just open our hearts to how things are. Truth is also *opanayiko*: it leads us to peace.

The truth, then, is that which can be experienced by each of us when we use our innate capacity to be awake. But this takes encouragement because there is such a strong tendency to avoid the painful and grasp at the comfortable. I feel gratitude that I've had the good fortune to meet beings who've been doing this kind of work and who encourage me, saying, 'You can do it. You don't have to believe in all those worries and fears. You can just listen to them. You can feel the sense that there is something terribly wrong and embrace that. You can trust in this capacity to be sensitive to how things are.' This is what a spiritual friend is.

I had the good fortune to come upon a group of people in Thailand twelve years ago who didn't make too big a problem of the puffed-up person who walked in through the door, but just encouraged me, saying, 'You can stay. Just make an effort to live harmlessly.' They didn't even ask me to like the monastery or to respect anybody. What allowed me to stay was just my willingness not to harm anything, to limit certain kinds of behaviour and just to be with whatever was going on. I was encouraged not to worry, and to get a feeling for all the gobbledegook of consciousness—the grubby stuff as well as the beautiful stuff— and to begin to be sensitive to the fact that it was changing just as the forest, the insects and the seasons were all changing. So, it's a great help when we are living with others who are inclining in a virtuous and reflective way.

In the same way, coming to this country where not many people appreciate the strange form that we Theravada Buddhist monks have, or the fact that we are mendicants, and to have encountered so much support, so much understanding—I'm very grateful for that too. Also that there are places like Sharpham and people like Maurice Ash who make available places where we can meet and bring presence of mind to these issues.

The attitude of being willing to learn from what arises in life and the sense of support we get from our spiritual friends allow us to welcome even the unpleasant things that come to us and to begin to see that our analysis of what is tragic, what is sad, is just an assumption too. In my own case, I had typhoid in Thailand, and I've also been struggling with Crohn's Disease these past ten years. At first it just seemed so unfortunate. A wrestling champion devastated by Crohn's Disease—boo hoo! But this is life! There is, of course, a tendency to moan, 'Why me?', but then we begin to wonder, 'Am I asking life not to be how it is?' How sensible is that? We can then become a little more humble and start to let go of our views about what is tragic and what is not.

In my own case I can say quite honestly that the illnesses that I have had have taught me that the things that I assumed were mine are not really mine. I used to have a great deal of will-power; it could crush just about anything—and then to find myself flattened, weak, with a mind that couldn't even think properly. But I've been incredibly grateful for the opportunity to learn to accept that, because if we attach to a limited condition, like energy or strength, then we will be frightened all the time because we are so vulnerable. Think of all the things that could happen to us. You can get nose diseases, eye diseases, skin diseases, tongue diseases, heart diseases, liver diseases—the whole works. I didn't know whether I'd be able to talk tonight because I get ulcers in my mouth from Crohn's Disease. So, if we identify with this body as 'me', then we really have to be careful; and even then we lose out because no matter how good we are at clinging, life shakes us off. You can't cling to anything without being shaken off. No way! In Buddhism, we use the word *dukkha* to describe the burning, the suffering that comes from resisting the way things are.

When we begin to bring presence of mind to this tendency to reject and grasp and resist, we also begin to see the fear and sadness and whatever that comes from that, and then an ease can come into our hearts too. I'll never forget being laid up in the monastery, useless and crazy in mind, yet realizing 'Everything is fine,' because there was a brightness there in the quality of being awake. That became so obvious. Sometimes too when we're parted from something really precious that we've identified with there's an opportunity for waking up to the deathless, to the source of it all: the unborn heart.

This sort of practice can sound very passive or like a cop-out —just accepting sickness, the dark side of life. But there are also all kinds of wonderful things that can be done, like practising loving-kindness. Who says that kind of practice doesn't have any effect on things? Try it and see what happens.

Recently, I was on the train to Newcastle with a new *anagarika* (postulant) who told me how much he resented people shouting 'Harry!!' after us. The Universe must have heard. At Sheffield, a big group of Sheffield Wednesday football fans got on, all drunk. Of course, they made a bee-line for us. I would love to give you a verbatim report on what happened but modesty prevents me repeating the language that was used; it was unbelievable.

There was a ringleader who was obviously respected. He was quick with his tongue, and he shouted from the other end of the carriage, 'Hey, Harry'—they thought we were Hare Krishna people.

And the other replied, 'Where's Harry? Anyone seen Harry? What about Larry?'

Eventually, if you'll pardon the expression, one of them sat his butt down on the table between Anagarika Andrew and myself. Meanwhile Andrew confided that he was thinking of climbing out the window. As for myself, I must admit I think it was the wrestler in me that came out; I'm a bit more used to being taunted.

Acting like nothing had happend, I just turned to the fellow and said, 'Would you like a seat?'

He was absolutely stunned. Then he started inquiring into the particulars of our sex life and things like that, offering their own colourful views and opinions.

After that another one shouted, 'Do you like niggers?'

I said, 'Well, I try to like all people.'

'Ah, come on,' they said, 'you must dislike something!'

I said, 'You're right, there is something I don't like. I don't like those things in myself which make me say and do things that I regret.'

And they went, 'Ohhhh, you mean like we're going to feel tomorrow morning?'

I said, 'You could put it that way.'

Then they started to reflect, 'You know, that's a very good answer,' and in about thirty minutes they started to calm down and we began in our own unique way to talk Dhamma. By the time those guys got off the train I was really touched.

'You take care of yourself now,' they said.

I got the feeling they would fight to the death if we were being attacked. And I didn't do anything but just make the effort not to follow my assumptions about who we were and who they were. Just allowing the heart to keep going around the situation without aversion created a possibility for dramatic change to take place. If I'd clung to the thought, 'I've got to get them to say I'm a nice guy,' then I'd have had a problem. I really had to accept the possibility we could get beaten up. But why do we trust our fears so much and put so little faith in our capacity to be open and kind and sensitive to life? By being awake and vigilant and kind we can let freedom happen. In this particular case, we could free those men from having to be guys who were obscene and just revving each other up. They got beyond that. And we got beyond our assumptions about tough drunks.

So we can look at the things we most resent or think most tragic and listen to those views and begin to envelop them with this quality of spirit or mindfulness or being aware. Then, bowing to the changing nature of those views rather than making them solid, there is the opportunity to allow our rigid assumptions to cease and then there can be a true waking up to *how it is* —which is being in the loo that doesn't work at Stonehenge, or being taunted on the Newcastle train, or in the classroom when you've made an effort and nobody responds, or when your hand is being held up and you're being praised. The willingness to see that this is how it is is not another fixed view but a sensitive openness to life.

I offer these thoughts for us to consider, and I do appreciate all the support you've given me over the past few years. Thank you.

Meditation on Yama
Michael Campbell

Knowing that this body is like a froth, knowing that its nature is that of a mirage, and breaking the flowery shafts of Mara, the disciple passes untouched by death.

Buddhist Scripture

Time to start thinking
About dark waters
Time to contemplate ends
Not 'half in love
With easeful death'
But just good friends.

Why assume cold and pain
A gallimaufry
Of monsters to dread?
Chief of these is Yama himself
And you can't fear him
When you're dead.

Time to take unfearful glances
Towards the unseen
Time to chat about things unsaid
We can plan the events of tomorrow
Consuming today with fear
But we can't see ahead.

MEDITATION ON YAMA

Look at the leaves in the wind
A sheep dead in the stream
Bones on the moor
Where are they off to
If not back to a place
They've been before?

Only two questions to ask
As the leaves fall
And clouds re-form
Who am I now?
And where was my original face
Before I was born?

... information about the Sharpham Conference Programme ... from The Administrator, Sharpham Conference ... House, Ashprington, Totnes, Devon TQ9 7UT.

The Sharpham Conference Programme

Buddhism in Britain (June '87) Stephen Batchelor
The Tibetan Way of Healing (February '88) Stephen Batchelor
Teaching Buddhism (March '88) Stephen Batchelor
Hindu-Buddhist Dialogue (July '88) S.Batchelor & Ranchor Prime
Towards a Buddhist Psychology (October '88) Stephen Batchelor
Shamanism (November '88) John Crook
Buddhism and World Peace (April '89) Stephen Batchelor
Language, Silence and Emptiness (July '89) Stephen Batchelor
Tradition and Authority (November '89) Christina Feldman
Being and Becoming (April '90 & April '91) Anne Bancroft
Krishnamurti: a Re-appraisal (May '90) B.Nicholson and John Crook
Ethics and Economics in Buddhism (June '90 & January '91)
    Stephen Batchelor
Buddhism and Cognitive Science (October '90) Guy Claxton
Green Spirituality (November '90) Satish Kumar
Education and Buddhism (June '92) Peter Carey
The Family and the Conundrum of the Solitary Spiritual Journey
    (October '92) Claire Ash Wheeler
Contemplation (November '92) Nick Scott

In addition to these events, which for the most part took the form of closed colloquia, a series of self-funding artists' workshops have been included in the Conference Programme.

Tape recordings and director's reports are available in the archives of the Sharpham Trust.

The Trust plans to issue a series of booklets summarizing the proceedings of selected colloquia.

Further information about the Sharpham Conference Programme can be obtained from: The Administrator, Sharpham Conference Programme, Sharpham House, Ashprington, Totnes, Devon TQ9 7UT, Devon.

Notes on the Contributors

MAURICE ASH took a degree in Economics at London School of Economics, then saw war service in the Western Desert, Italy and Greece. Aside from a continuing involvement in farming, his own attempts to form a comprehensive theory of society were brought to an abrupt end by his first contact with Wittgenstein's philosophy in the 1950s, which demonstrated the impossibility of the task he has set himself. Since then he has attempted to write his book in deeds rather than words and has been Chairman of the Town and Country Planning Association, of Dartington Hall Trust, of the Green Alliance and of the Sharpham Trust. His books include *New Renaissance* (1987) and *Journey Through the Eye of a Needle* (1989).

STEPHEN BATCHELOR was born in Scotland in 1953 and in 1972 travelled to India. From 1974 he spent ten years as a Buddhist monk in the Tibetan and Zen traditions, living in India, Switzerland, Germany and Korea. He is the translator of Shantideva's *Guide to the Bodhisattva's Way of Life* and author of *Alone with Others: An Existential Approach to Buddhism*, the *Tibet Guide*, which won the Thomas Cook Guide Book Award in 1988, and *The Faith to Doubt*. He is a Buddhist chaplain in Channings Wood Prison, a conference director for the Sharpham Trust, an associate faculty member of the Schumacher College and a former member of the Sharpham North Community.

MICHAEL CAMPBELL was a teacher at various schools, including Dartington Hall, and latterly a writer and radio dramatist. He also in 1985 presented the BBC Radio 4 feature 'The Lotus and the Lion' on Buddhism in Britain. A friend of Sharpham, he died in 1989.

JOHN CROOK was until recently Reader in Ethology at the University of Bristol. He has also travelled and researched in Ladakh. He first became interested in Buddhism in Hong Kong in the early 1950s, where he met Shi Yang-yen, a disciple of Ch'an Master Hsu-yun (Xu Yun). After practising meditation in California, at Samyé Ling in Scotland and at Throssel Hole Priory in Cumbria, he trained in Berner's 'Enlightenment Intensive' with Jeff Love and for the last fifteen years has led Western Zen Retreats, which are an amalgam of Berner's 'communication exercise' and traditional zazen. He has recently been studying with Ch'an Master Sheng-yen in New York. His books include *The Evolution of Human Consciousness* (1980).

SOPHIE DAY completed a doctorate on Ladakhi possession ritual in 1989 (University of London). She is currently a research associate in the Department of Anthropology, LSE, and an honorary research fellow in the Academic Department, Public Health, St Mary's Hospital Medical School.

GAI EATON was born in Switzerland and educated at Charterhouse and King's, Cambridge. After working for many years as a journalist, he embraced Islam in 1951 in Egypt, then joined the British Diplomatic Service. More lately he has been Consultant to the Islamic Cultural Centre in London. He is the author of *King of the Castle* (1978) and *Islam and the Destiny of Man* (1985).

SHENPEN HOOKHAM has trained in the Kagyu-Nyingma tradition of Tibetan Buddhism since 1969. She spent five and a half years in India and four years in Europe as a Buddhist nun/translator/interpreter. She is the author of *The Buddha Within*, a study of the Tathagatagarbha doctrine. An assistant teacher with the Longchen Foundation, she is married to Michael Hookham.

KEN JONES has practised Zen Buddhism since 1979 and has been involved in Buddhist groups in Leeds, Harrogate and Aberystwyth. He has also been a prison chaplain and done interfaith work. His special interest lies in socially-engaged Buddhism. He is a prominent member of the British arm of the Network of Engaged Buddhists and is the author of *The Social Face of Buddhism: An Approach to Social and Political Activism*, as well as numerous articles and pamphlets.

AJAHN KITTISARO (RANDOLPH WEINBERG) grew up in Tennessee and attended both Princeton and Oxford universities. In 1976 he travelled to Thailand and entered a Buddhist monastery of the Theravada Forest Tradition, being ordained a bhikkhu the following year. In 1978 he came to Chithurst Forest Monastery in West Sussex and between 1986 and 1988 was Senior Monk at the Devon Vihara near Honiton. He has recently disrobed.

SATISH KUMAR is the Director of the newly-formed Schumacher College which is an international centre for the study of global ecology and spiritual values, based at Dartington in Devon. He is also the Editor of

Resurgence magazine which was described by *The Guardian* as 'the artistic and spiritual flagship of the eco-movement'.

JAMES LOW is an art therapist and psychotherapist working at the Middlesex Hospital in London. A longstanding practitioner of Buddhism, attached specifically to the Tibetan Nyingma school, he has led art and meditation groups for many years.

MARTIN PALMER is Director of ICOREC (International Consultancy of Religion, Education and Culture) based in Manchester, a Christian theologian and student of Chinese.

JONATHON PORRITT, former Director of Friends of the Earth and Chairman of the Green Party, is a leading spokesman and broadcaster on Green issues. He is the author of *Seeing Green* and *Save the Earth*.

HARRY RUTHERFORD, who died in 1991, was a trustee of the New Atlantis Foundation. He worked for many years with the Yugoslav savant Dimitrije Mitrinović and his circle (which during the 'Thirties included Alan Watts). He was also the editor of *Certainly Future*(1987), a selection of Mitrinović's writings.

JOHN SNELLING was a writer and broadcaster specializing in Buddhist and Central Asian matters. He died in January 1992 just before *Sharpham Miscellany* went to press. A member of the Sharpham North Community, he was working on *Agvan Dorzhiev and the Saga of Buddhism in Russia*, due to be published in 1992. His books include *The Sacred Mountain* (1983), *The Buddhist Handbook* (1987) and *The Elements of Buddhism* (1990), as well as eight books for children on Buddhism and mythology. He also edited two volumes of the early writings of Alan Watts.

MAURICE WALSHE is the translator of both the sermons of Meister Eckhart and of the *Digha Nikaya*, an important collection of early Buddhist suttas (published under the title *Thus Have I Heard*). He is also the author of *Medieval German Literature: A Survey* and *A Middle High German Reader*. In 1979 he retired as Reader in German and Deputy Director of the Institute of Germanic Studies, University of London. For a few months in 1989 he was an ordained Theravada Buddhist monk.